THE WORLD OF SCIENCE
YOUR BODY

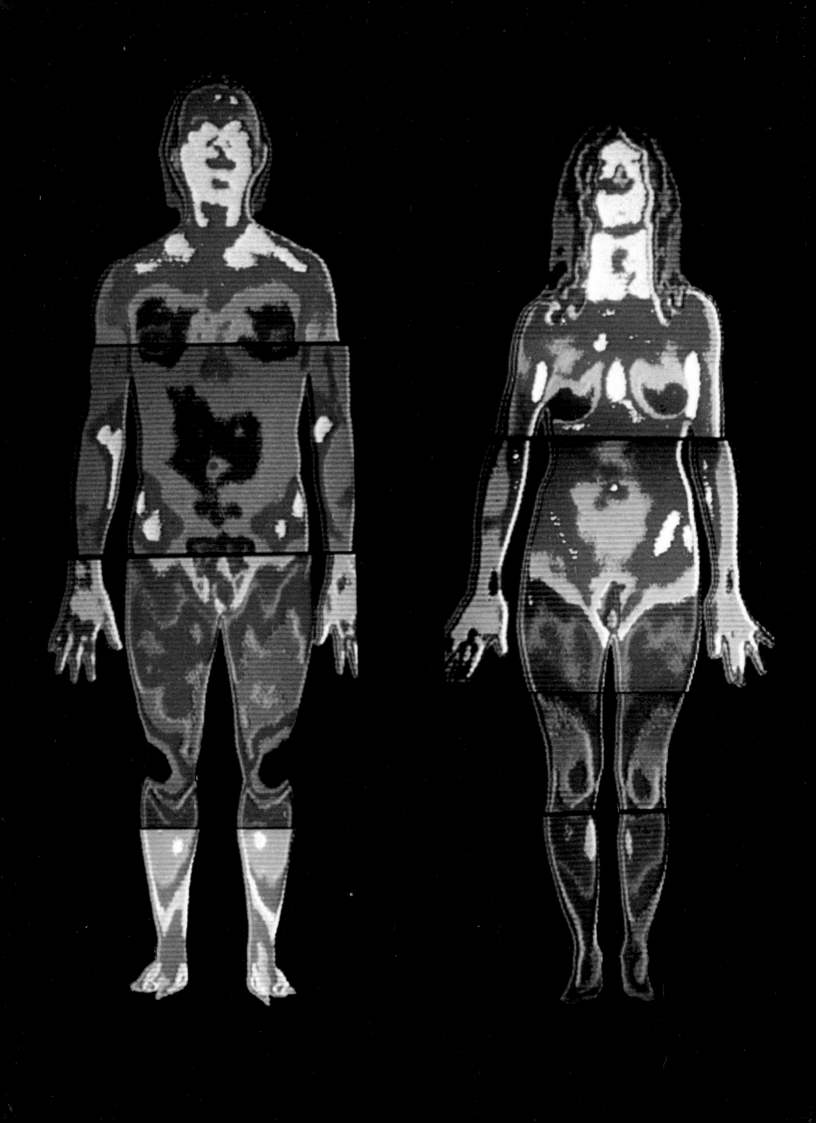

THE WORLD OF SCIENCE
YOUR BODY

IRENE FEKETE & PETER DORRINGTON WARD

Facts On File Publications
New York, New York ● Bicester, England

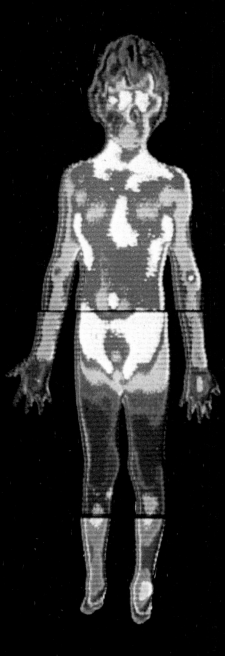

YOUR BODY

**Library of Congress Cataloging in Publication
Data**

Main entry under title:

The world of science.

   Includes index.
   Summary: A twenty-five volume encyclopedia of
scientific subjects, designed for eight- to twelve-year-
olds. One volume is entirely devoted to projects.
   1. Science—Dictionaries, Juvenile.   1. Science—
Dictionaries
Q121.J86   1984   500   84-1654

ISBN: 0-87196-989-0

Printed in Yugoslavia
10 9 8 7 6 5 4 3 2

Previous pages
Thermograph of a
man, a woman and a
boy.

Consultant editors
Eleanor Felder, former managing editor, *New Book of
Knowledge*
James Neujahr, Dean of the School of Education, City
College of New York
Ethan Signer, Professor of Biology, Massachusetts
Institute of Technolgy
J. Tuzo Wilson, Director General, Ontario Science
Centre

Editor Penny Clarke
Designer Roger Kohn

CONTENTS

▲Bjorn Borg, one of the world's greatest tennis players in action.

Note There are some unusual words in this book. They are explained in the Glossary on page 62. The first time each word is used in the text it is printed in *italics*.

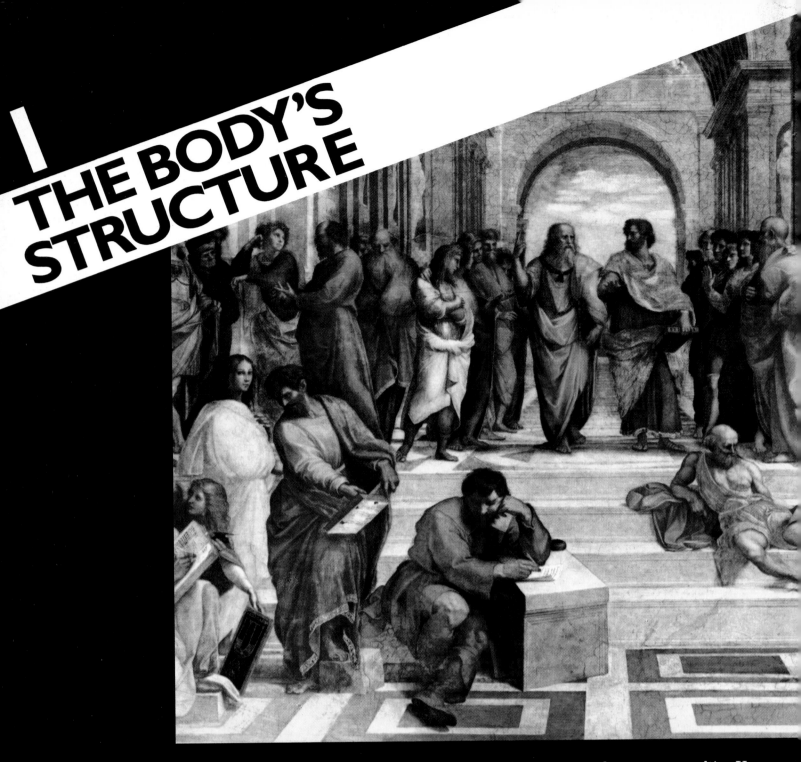

ASKING QUESTIONS

Everyone likes asking questions. What is this? How does it work? What is it like inside? Why does it change? What will happen next? People have always asked questions like this, especially about their own bodies. Probably you have noticed that questions often come into your head when you are thinking about something else. Watching a kitten chase its tail you start to wonder if people ever had tails. Bored and miserable because you are home from school with the measles, you suddenly begin to wonder how those itchy red spots popped out on your skin. You then go on to think about skin in general. Why is your forehead smooth, except when you frown, and your grandmother's wrinkled all the time, even when she is smiling? When you cut your finger or graze your knee, blood comes out. It is bright red at first and then goes brown. You stop bleeding. The cut heals. In a few days you can hardly see where it was. This seems puzzling and mysterious.

The Father of Anatomy
Two thousand five hundred years ago in ancient Greece people were beginning to look for answers to the sort of questions

◀Aristotle (centre left) is shown in this painting teaching a group of students. They are not working in a laboratory but in the porch of a great government building. He had virtually no equipment but his students learned how to compare the way plants, animals and human beings live and grow. His methods were a model for most scientific investigation until modern times.

which might occur to you. By carefully and accurately examining, describing, and comparing what they saw, they began to transform curiosity into science. The first important steps were taken by a Greek named Aristotle who taught in Athens three hundred and fifty years before the birth of Christ. Aristotle guessed that if he carefully observed the way animals and fish live then cut open their dead bodies, he would find clues to how a human body was made. Cutting into bodies to expose the inside parts is called *dissection*. Even today when scientists have such wonderful *instruments* as microscopes to help them

study very small pieces taken from plants, animals or human bodies, dissection is still important. It is the basic skill needed by anyone who studies *anatomy*, the science which explains how living things are put together.

Because of his pioneering work, Aristotle is often called the Father of Anatomy. Twenty-two years after he died, a scientist in Egypt received permission to dissect the body of a criminal who had been executed. Until then, no one had been allowed to work on a dead human body. With the public dissection in Alexandria, Egypt, human anatomy as a scientific study began.

ANATOMY – DISCOVERING THE HUMAN BODY

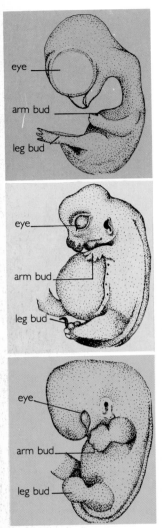

▲These three tiny unborn creatures look almost the same, but scientists know they are not. At the top is a week-old chick. Chickens develop fast and in two weeks it will be ready to hatch. In the middle is a three-week-old pig. Growing more slowly, it will need 16 more weeks inside its mother. The bottom picture shows a five-week-old unborn baby, an embryo. It must stay inside its mother another 33 weeks before it is ready to be born.

After such a promising beginning in Greece and Egypt, anatomy made little progress for fourteen hundred years. During this time doctors and scientists in Europe were not allowed to dissect dead bodies. People thought it was evil to make use of a body in any way, even to help others. The word anatomy comes from Greek and means 'to cut'. Because they were forbidden to cut up bodies and examine them directly, doctors and scientists had to make use of information handed down over the centuries from the Greeks long ago. Often mistakes crept in and were reported as fact.

In the sixteenth century the laws began to change. Dissection was permitted in some places. Andreas Vesalius, a Belgian, travelled from Brussels to the University of Padua, in Italy. There he took advantage of the new ideas to produce the first complete and accurate description of the human body. All his superb drawings were based on dissections he performed himself. These drawings inspired artists as well as doctors and scientists. They too began to study anatomy seriously. Today anatomy often plays a part in an artist's training.

The first microscope

One hundred years after Vesalius, a Dutch scientist, Anton van Leewenhoek, invented the microscope. This was a wonderful instrument for many different kinds of scientist but was particularly helpful for studying the body. We know that the brain and heart are made up of many smaller parts or structures. The microscope made it possible for us to see things that are so small they are invisible to the naked eye.

Modern aids for anatomy

Today we have even more powerful aids than the simple light microscope. We have, among many others, *electron* microscopes, X-rays and ultrasound scanners. Electron microscopes use bursts of energy instead of light to give a picture of things far too small to be seen even by the most powerful light microscope. X-rays use a combination of energy and

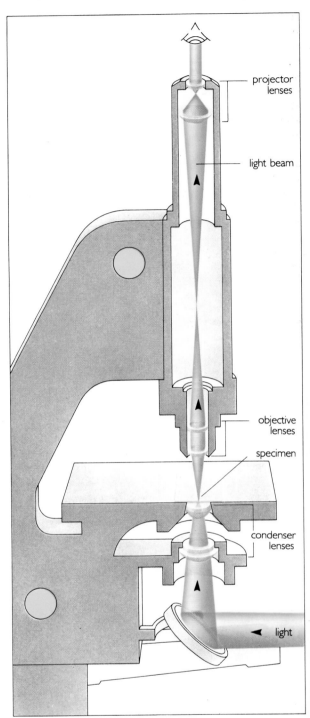

photography. They take a picture through the skin of what is happening inside us. Ultrasound is one of the newest methods. Special sound waves pass through the skin. They then bounce back from the brain, or heart, or whatever is being examined. Suddenly, on a television screen connected to the scanner, we see a moving picture of what is going on inside our body as it is actually happening.

◀A microscope is an important instrument in studying parts of the body. This is a standard light microscope. Its lenses, small pieces of curved glass, bend light in such a way that tiny structures on the surface or within the body can be enlarged. A small sample, called the specimen, is put on a thin piece of glass. The objective lens magnifies the image, perhaps more than 10,000 times. The projector lens enlarges the image even more and projects it up to the eye.

▲Cells from the part of the brain called the cerebellum (see page 34). The big cells are called Purkinje cells after Johannes Purkinje who discovered them. He was one of the first scientists to study cells through a microscope.

◀This picture is part of a tendon seen through a polarising microscope – a very special microscope.

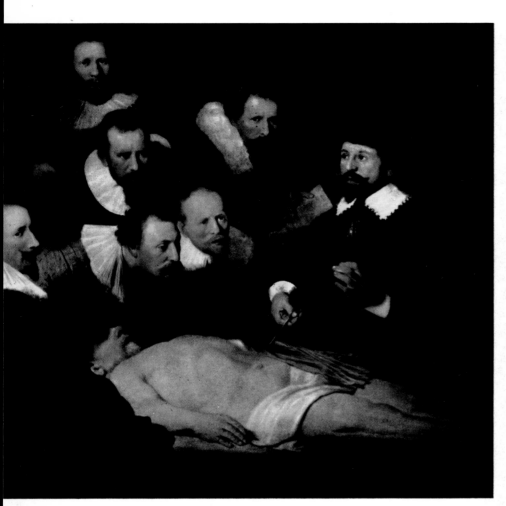

PHYSIOLOGY – HOW THE BODY WORKS

Finding out just what is under our skin and describing it perfectly will answer some but not all of our questions. We also want to know how things link up and work together. This sort of information is sometimes difficult to get. People studying the human body have often had to wait until other scientists invented special instruments or machines before making further investigations. But joining all available information together is vital. Explaining the way special parts of a living thing actually do their work is the science of *physiology*. Anatomy and physiology both now make up the basic training for medical professions everywhere.

William Harvey discovers the blood system
In 1628, an English doctor, William Harvey, became very interested in the heart and blood. At that time people

▲Nicholaas Tulp (right), a great Dutch teacher of anatomy, has peeled back the skin on a dead man's left arm. He is showing his students in 17th-century Holland what the muscles look like.

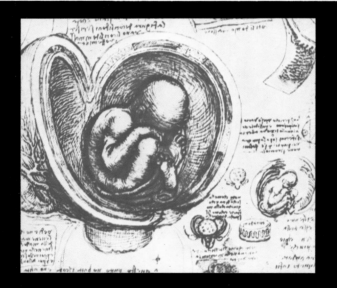

▲A precise sketch of the way a baby is curled up inside its mother before it is born was done by Leonardo da Vinci. This great artist thought scientific study was as important as art and learned how to dissect the human body.

▶This clear drawing of the muscles which lie just below a man's skin was made by Vesalius in 1543. Accurate pictures like this were an enormous help to doctors.

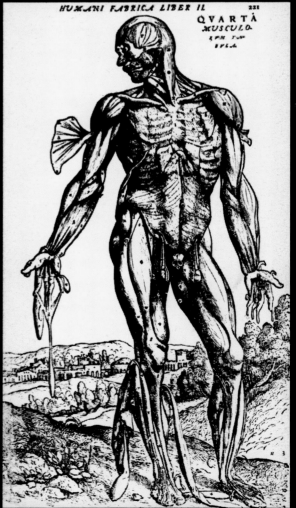

thought that although blood could be found in some tubes inside us, mostly it just seeped through the body like water in a sponge. Harvey noticed when he dissected a body, however, that the heart looked like a small pump. He also observed thousands and thousands of connecting tubes, some large and some so small he could hardly see them, reaching into every part of the body. When he tied a cloth tightly around a living man's upper arm, he saw one of these tubes which carried blood, a *vein*, stand out clearly under the man's skin. By touching the vein very gently he discovered he could feel the blood moving inside it. He could even tell in which direction it was flowing. Slowly he put together all these facts. The heart really was a pump. All the blood carrying tubes within the body made up a great connected circulation system in which blood moved constantly round and round the body.

The body's other systems
Encouraged by Harvey's discovery, other doctors and scientists looked for and found the links between special parts of the body, our *organs*, and basic activities like eating, breathing, growing, moving, and having babies. Groups of organs were studied together and described as *systems*.

In a period of about two hundred years we discovered the main facts about most of our body's systems. We learned that breathing in and out is controlled by the *respiratory* system. This includes our mouth, nose, windpipe, a tough muscle in the middle of our body called the diaphragm, our lungs and ribs. Our *digestive* system, which changes food into the energy we need to live, has many parts too. The most important are the stomach and a long coil of connecting tubes, the intestines. Whether we are a boy or girl depends on which *reproductive* system we have. A girl's reproductive system has organs which produce eggs that can grow into babies. A boy's reproductive system produces the seed which is necessary to make the girl's egg grow. Our *nervous* system links our brain to all parts of the body and it is the key to how we see, hear, talk, feel and move.

▼X-rays and modern colour photography can show us detail inside the human body when it is still alive. We can see the bones in the boxer's skull, his teeth and neck very clearly. We can see the small finger bones in the clenched fist of the man who is hitting him.

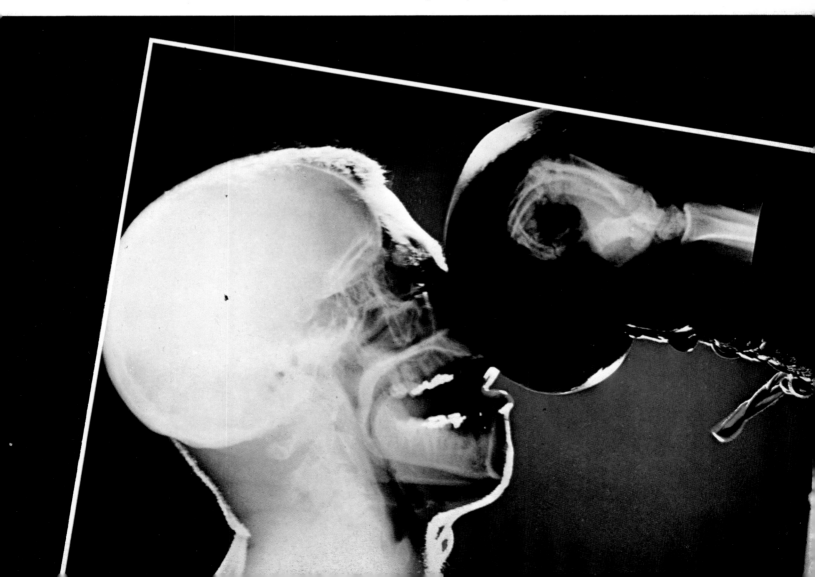

CELLS – THE BODY'S BUILDING BLOCKS

What would you guess is the tiniest part of your body? An eyelash? An invisible tube deep inside your finger carrying blood to its tip? A tiny pump on your skin? No, none of these. The smallest part of the body is a single *cell*. There are about 1,000 million million cells in an adult human body. There are all sorts of cells and each kind groups together to form tissues. The tissues can group together to form organs like our brain, stomach, heart and lungs or structures like our bones.

A cell is a minute blob of jelly-like material surrounded by a thin envelope, its *membrane*. Even though a cell is so tiny, it can have many parts all of which can be busy doing things. The cell is the basic unit of life but under the microscope it can seem like a busy city. All living things, plants, animals and people, are made up of cells. Healthy cells work together in harmony, doing whatever their special job is. When more cells are needed, a cell splits and can produce two or more cells exactly like itself.

All cells, whatever their type, have three main parts: a membrane to hold it together, cytoplasm which makes up its body, and a nucleus to direct its work. The membrane is a very special kind of

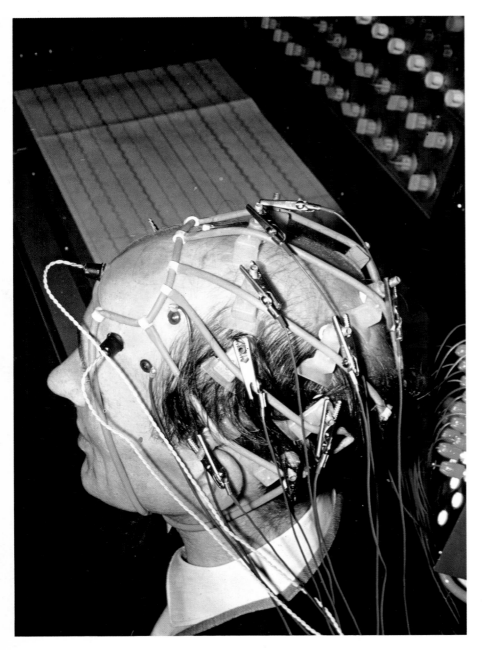

▲Because the brain is such a complicated organ and is completely shielded by the hard bones of our skull, physiologists have had to wait a long time to find out how it really works. The wires attached to the man's head are capable of picking up very faint electrical signals. They can read the brain's signals just as if they were a radio broadcast in code. Now we can learn which parts of the brain control which parts of the body.

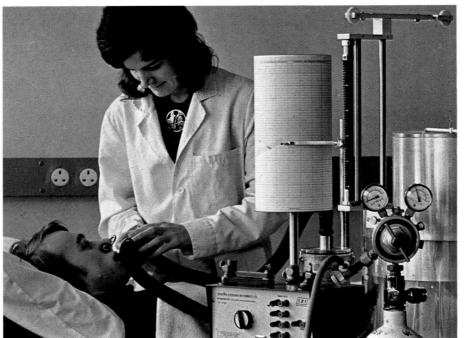

◄A young man is co-operating in a test to find out more about how the respiratory system works. He is breathing in and out through two black tubes which are connected to new scientific equipment. The automatic pencil moving across the drum in the centre of the picture is marking down just how much oxygen – the gas we all need to live – he is taking out of the air and into his lungs.

◄All living organisms are made up of cells. As you can see from this picture and the others on this page, cells come in many different shapes and sizes. Each different cell has a different function.

▼Cells are so small that it is difficult to find out what is in them. So, to help show up the different structures inside a cell, scientists use special dyes or stains. These cells have been stained with a special orange dye to show up fat.

►A cross section or a slice through the tissue inside your nose would, under a microscope, show you that it was made up of many different types of cells. The large ones in the middle are gland cells which make mucus, the sticky fluid we blow out when we have a cold.

◀Plants too can help us learn about ourselves. Because all living things have many activities in common, plants and animals can often tell us what substances may harm us or help us in some way. Here a girl is checking to see which group of seeds, each treated in a different way, is growing best.

envelope. It can select what substances come into and out of the cell. The cytoplasm is the greyish jelly which fills the cell but it can have in it all sorts of structures and even small sacs holding pigments to colour it, depending on what kind of cell it is. The nucleus is like a control board and it is particularly important when the cell divides. It instructs the dividing cell so new ones are perfect copies of the original.

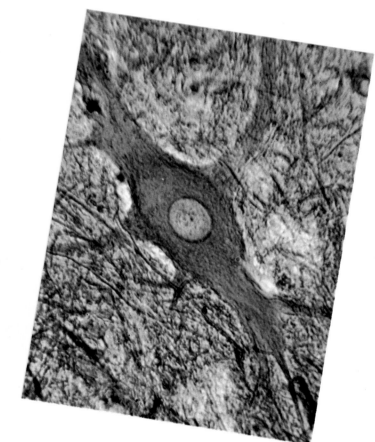

▲A single nerve cell taken from inside a human spinal cord and magnified 2,000 times looks like this. Nerve cells like this carry messages from the brain to the muscles.

▶At the top of the diagram (**opposite**) the artist has drawn seven different types of cell (A–G), and then, taking features from them all, has put together a giant imaginary cell so you can see just how different cells can be and how many things can be inside them.

A A plant cell

B A nerve cell in the brain

C A long cell that could line either the inside of your throat or part of your intestines

D Another sort of brain cell. This one would support and feed cells like 'B'

E This cell contains a special juice to digest food

F A muscle cell can change its shape easily

G A skin cell containing blobs of colour

1 The cell membrane connects directly to another envelope inside, the membrane around the nucleus

2 The nucleus of the cell, with its own powerhouse (2a)

3 Mitochondria provide the energy for the cell

4 Some holes and sacs within the cell are empty, others store whatever the cell is making

5 Some structures make proteins, the basic material for all living matter

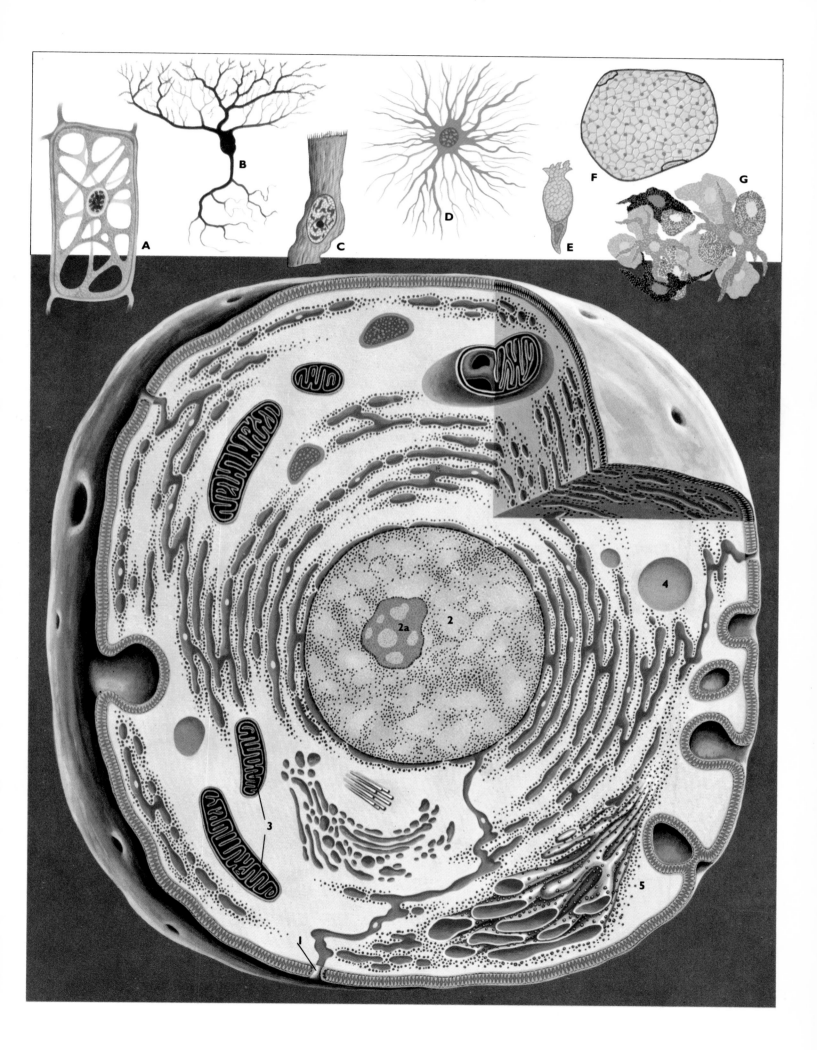

A

B

C

D

E

F

G

2a 2

4

3

1

5

15

BONES AND JOINTS

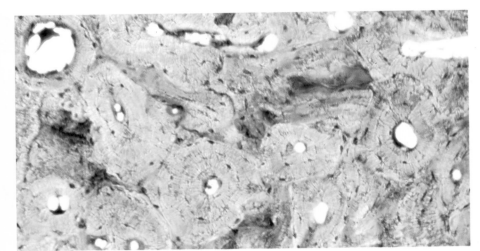

Sometimes cartilage in the joints becomes diseased. This is called arthritis and when this happens, movement becomes difficult and painful.

◄A photograph from a microscope of a slice through a piece of hard bone shows the tubes of the Haversian canals as white holes with darker bone cells around them.

▼An X-ray photograph of the bones in a normal human hand.

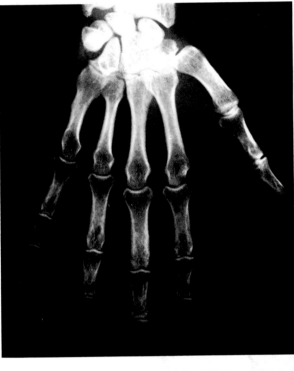

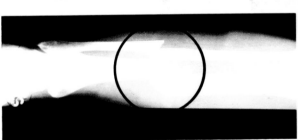

▲An X-ray photograph showing a broken leg. The bones will have to be pulled back into their correct position to heal.

range of movement

range of movement

▲The human elbow at the top works very much like the artificial ball and socket joint below.

Bone is a very hard living tissue which grows and repairs itself when injured. The bones of people or animals which we may see in museums are the hard mineral remains of once-living bones. When alive, bones contain softer material as well. Some of it is called red marrow and makes new red cells for the blood. Bones give bodies their basic shape and strength. There are about 230 bones in the human body. These make up the skeleton. Some bones protect delicate organs from damage. The skull protects the brain, the ribs protect our heart and lungs. Other bones enable us to move.

Where one bone meets another, there is always a joint of some kind. Some joints are completely immobile after we have stopped growing. The thin hair lines on a skull are really joints showing where the different bones of the skull join. Joints between the many small bones in the spine rest on little cushions called discs. These are made of cartilage, a springy substance that can be pressed down or twisted but will always return to its original shape. Thus we can bend and twist our spines easily but have problems if any of the little discs slip out of place.

Because we make big movements with our arms and legs, they have special joints. A bone 'ball' fits into a round hole or 'socket' called the synovial cavity. That hole is filled with a fluid to help the ball move easily. The knee is a simple joint and works like a hinge. The elbow is a more complicated hinge-and-pivot joint so we can bend and twist our forearms.

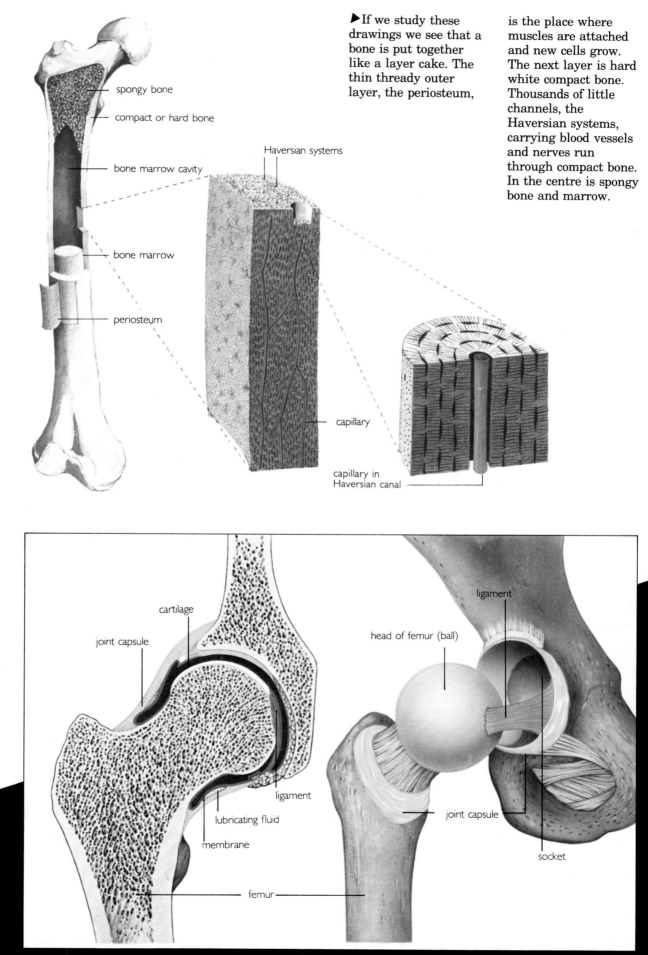

spongy bone

compact or hard bone

bone marrow cavity

bone marrow

periosteum

Haversian systems

capillary

capillary in
Haversian canal

►If we study these drawings we see that a bone is put together like a layer cake. The thin thready outer layer, the periosteum, is the place where muscles are attached and new cells grow. The next layer is hard white compact bone. Thousands of little channels, the Haversian systems, carrying blood vessels and nerves run through compact bone. In the centre is spongy bone and marrow.

►Two drawings show clearly how a hip joint works. On the left is the thigh bone in its socket. On the right are the bones themselves, showing how the joint is formed and how ligaments hold it together.

joint capsule

cartilage

ligament

lubricating fluid

membrane

femur

head of femur (ball)

ligament

joint capsule

socket

HEART AND LUNGS

The heart and lungs are important organs working together to put oxygen into the blood, take carbon dioxide out of it, and keep blood moving so all the cells in the body can stay alive. The heart is a living pump about the size of a tightly closed fist. It has four chambers. On the right side, it takes in deoxygenated blood. This is the term for blood that has given up its oxygen to the cells on its journey around the body. This blood has reached the heart through tubes called veins. The heart pushes deoxygenated blood into the lungs. The lungs exchange carbon dioxide for oxygen which is taken up into the blood. This oxygenated blood then goes back into the chambers of the heart on the left side. The heart then pushes the fresh blood out into the body along other tubes called arteries. In less than a minute, all the blood in your body makes a round trip from your head to your toes and back again, passing through your heart and lungs.

If you bend your arm up and down to a steady beat, you have to think in order to make the muscles work. The heart is a muscle but unlike other muscles in your body, it has a built-in rhythm. It contracts and expands steadily without any help. The heart beats about seventy times a minute and has only half a second of rest between beats.

The lungs
The lungs are made of a special stretchy

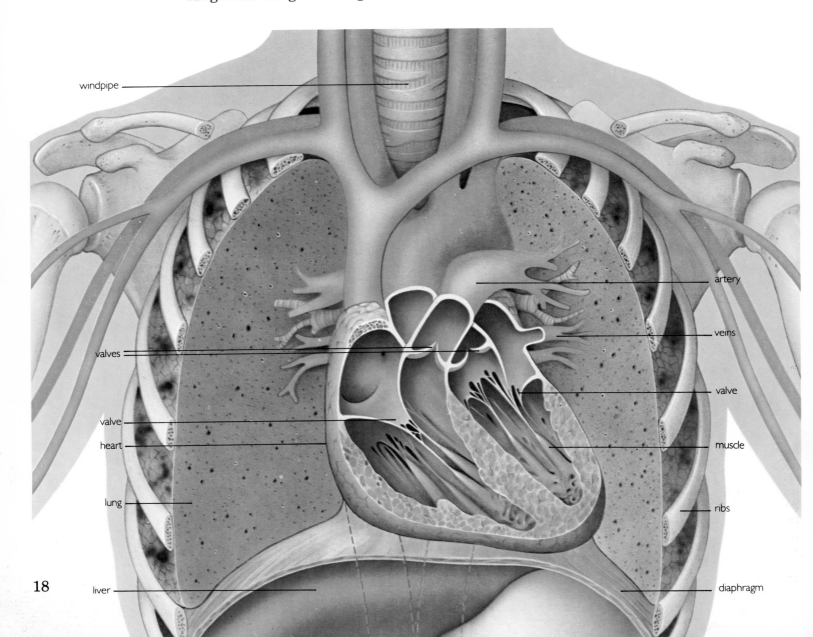

windpipe

valves

valve

heart

lung

liver

artery

veins

valve

muscle

ribs

diaphragm

tissue, very different from the heart muscle. The lungs do not expand and contract on their own. A very thick muscle called the diaphragm stretches across under the bottom of the lungs. As this moves up and down it makes your ribs go in and out so you take in oxygen and breathe out carbon dioxide. The air you breathe in travels down a series of pipes that get smaller and smaller until they reach the tiny air sacs called alveoli. This is where the exchange of gases in the blood takes place. Usually the lungs move in and out about fifteen or twenty times a minute.

An important partnership
The heart and lungs work more quickly if you are doing something very active.

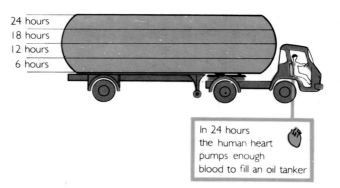

In 24 hours the human heart pumps enough blood to fill an oil tanker

When you rest or sleep the rhythm slows down but never stops. This partnership of the heart and lungs is one of the most important in the body. How it is working can give a doctor many clues about your health. This is why listening to the heart-beat and breathing is a basic part of any health check-up.

◀The heart is a powerful muscle. You have 6–7 litres (5–6 quarts) of blood in your body and your heart pushes them round the body through 100,000 km (over 60,000 miles) of blood vessels.

▼Each lung is made up of hundreds of air sacs or alveoli. Each one is surrounded by a network of blood vessels; carbon dioxide passes out of the blood they carry and oxygen is absorbed into it.

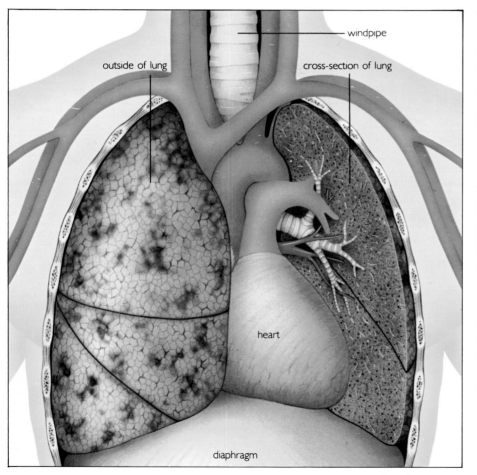

windpipe
outside of lung
cross-section of lung
heart
diaphragm

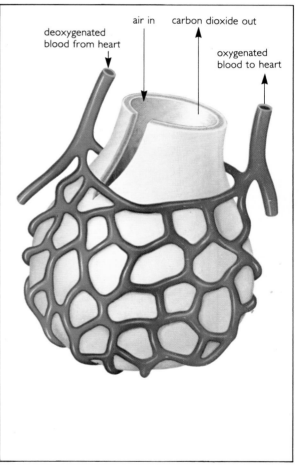

deoxygenated blood from heart
air in
carbon dioxide out
oxygenated blood to heart

◀A heart beat begins in the top right chamber and then spreads through the heart like ripples on a pond. The valves are one-way-only gates in the heart to make sure that blood does not leak back. Oxygenated and deoxygenated blood never mix in a healthy heart.

▲Air, containing oxygen, moves down the windpipe in the throat into the lungs as we breathe in. Air, containing carbon dioxide, goes up as we breathe out.

▶The arteries and veins are connected by tiny tubes called capillaries. This drawing shows just how the oxygenated blood comes to the end of its circuit and begins to go back to the heart as deoxygenated blood.

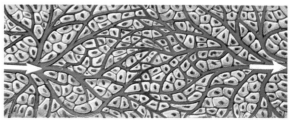

BLOOD AND ITS WORK

▶William Harvey (1578–1657) was the first person to describe correctly the way the blood circulates round the body. In this picture he is explaining his work to King Charles I (who is seated) and his son, the future king of England, Charles II.

Strange as it may seem, scientists call blood a tissue too, like bone. This is because blood is a group of special cells doing very important tasks within the body. Unlike bone, blood is not in one special place but moves constantly through all parts of the body. But like bone it is made up of different types of cell.

An adult human usually has between 4.5 to 7 litres (4 to 6 quarts) of blood constantly moving around his body. Fifty-five per cent of this is a colourless fluid called plasma. The rest is made up of cells. The red cells, which give blood its colour, contain haemoglobin. This is the substance that makes it possible for blood cells to pick up and carry oxygen. White cells are colourless like plasma.

The body's transport system
Blood is the main transport service of the body. It also carries chemical messages and can defend the body against disease. Pushed along by the steady beating of the heart, blood passes through the lungs at the beginning of a circuit. There it picks up fresh *oxygen*, the *gas* all cells need to live. As it moves, it exchanges oxygen for *carbon dioxide* in the cells it passes. Carbon dioxide is the poisonous gas made by cells as they change food into energy. When the blood returns to the lungs, it leaves this behind and takes a new load of oxygen. We breathe out carbon dioxide and breath in oxygen.

When blood moves through the *intestines*, it picks up food and water to nourish the cells. As it passes through the *glands*, it picks up chemicals, *hormones*, which, in other parts of the body, will trigger all sorts of activity.

Protecting the body
The blood's other important job is to fight off infection, that is to destroy any virus or bacteria trying to harm the body. White cells in the blood surround harmful substances and destroy them. This is why we see pus in an infected cut. That nasty

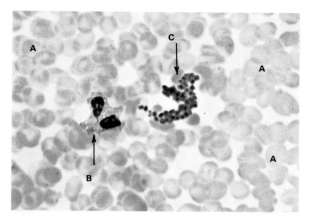

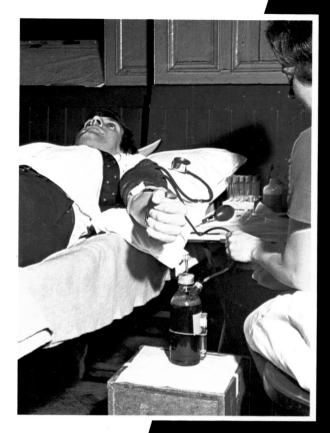

◀Sometimes when people are ill or injure[d] they need blood from another person to help them get better. Bloo[d] is carefully tested so that a person receive[s] only the sort of blood which will match his own. Giving blood is a[n] easy and painless way of helping others.

▲This is what human blood looks like if it is magnified 600 times, although the colour difference is now not too clear. The red cells (**A**) are far more numerous than the white cells (**B**). The platelets (**C**) are quite small and have formed a small group.

▼Red blood cells are large and flat, and their shape makes it easier for them to pick up and exchange oxygen as they move. Each cell lives about 120 days and makes 50,000 trips from the heart around the body.

▼Most blood cells are made in the marrow i[n] the centre of our bone[s.] It is thought that they all come from one cell which then divides int[o] five types.

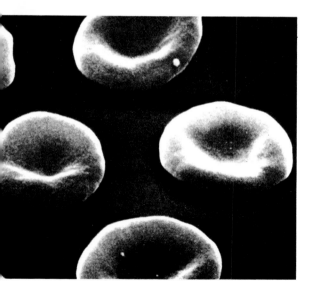

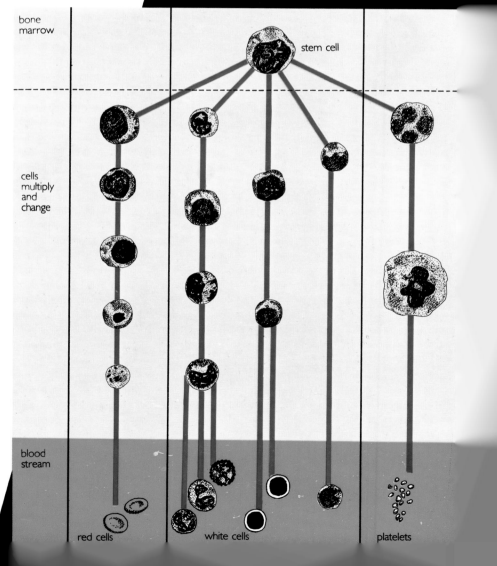

substance is the visible proof of blood battling to protect the body. It is made up of white blood cells, the watery part of the blood called plasma and the germs that the white cells have killed. White cells can also increase at a tremendous rate when we are ill, defending the body against harmful germs.

Platelets are the smallest cells in the blood. When we cut ourselves or are injured in some way, they rush to the spot, release a special chemical which helps form a kind of net within the blood and gradually, as other cells are trapped,

bone marrow

stem cell

cells multiply and change

blood stream

red cells

white cells

platelets

HOW THE LYMPH SYSTEM WORKS

Most of us know that blood is essential to life but our bodies contain another equally important fluid, lymph. It is a colourless, watery fluid that bathes and feeds the cells. It fills the spaces between groups of tissues and is made of water, white cells from the blood, digested food and waste.

The smallest tubes or vessels carrying blood are called capillaries. Their walls are so thin that liquid can pass through them easily. This is the way nourishment gets from the blood to the cells.

Sometimes, some of the food does not reach the cells but is trapped between the tissues. If it stayed there it would be harmful, so lymph washes it away. Lymph moves through the body in its own special channels. These channels contain valves, to make the lymph flow in only one direction.

Unlike blood, lymph does not have a pump. It moves as our muscles stretch and bend. If we stand absolutely still for a very long time, we may notice that our ankles swell, becoming white and puffy. This is because lymph has collected in them and needs to be moved along.

The tonsils – important lymph glands

As lymph moves inside the body, it passes through many groups of spongy tissue, the lymph nodes or glands. They are filters that take out any harmful germs or waste the lymph has collected. We have many lymph glands in our body and they are very important in keeping us healthy. There are groups of them in our armpits, in our neck and the inside top of our thighs, our groin. There are also some at the top and bottom of the back and our throat, our tonsils. These are the lymph nodes we hear about most often. Because of where they are, they are very active in trapping germs. Like other lymph nodes they produce lymphocytes, special cells that are very active in fighting infection. They also make substances called antibodies to help fight disease.

If they become inflamed, swollen and painful, causing a sore throat, we have a disease called tonsillitis. If a child gets it too often, the doctor may decide that the tonsils must be removed. Their work then is done by the remaining lymph glands.

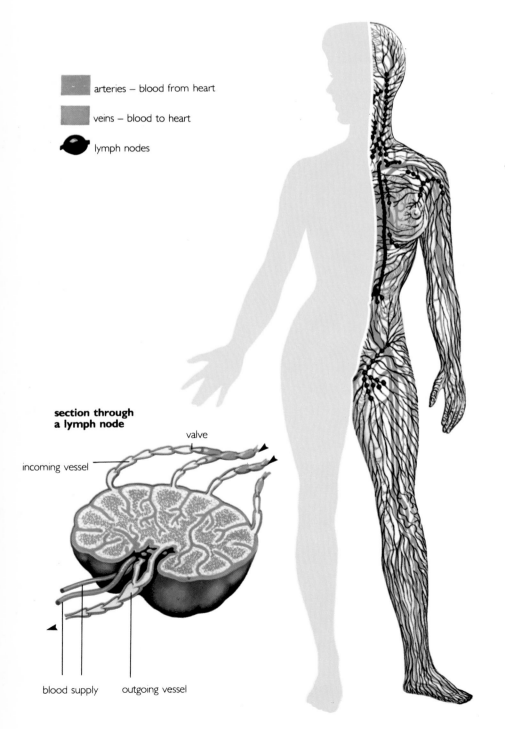

arteries – blood from heart

veins – blood to heart

lymph nodes

section through a lymph node

valve

incoming vessel

blood supply   outgoing vessel

◄If you think of all the fluid-carrying tubes in the body as a very complicated road map you will understand how they work. Blood goes round and round and is cleaned when it passes through the heart and lungs.

Lymph is purified when it goes through its filters, the nodes. The drawing shows us how a node works. The little gates or valves in the tubes make certain the lymph moves only in the right direction.

nose cavity   adenoids

tonsil

tongue   tonsil

◀ This section through the head shows three groups of tonsils, including the adenoids. They are all part of the lymph system and help the body fight disease.

▶ Removing a tonsil is a very simple operation. The doctor uses this instrument called a tonsillotome. It easily reaches into the back of the throat, snips off the tonsil like a leaf and then keeps hold of it until it is taken out of the mouth.

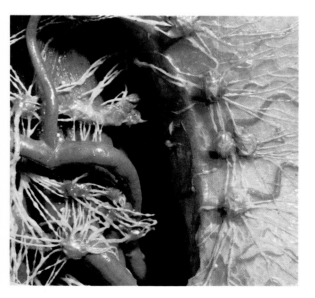

◀ An artist's plastic model of part of the liver (on the left) and the stomach (on the right) shows clearly the blood vessels and the lymph vessels and nodes. The blood vessels are the red tubes and the lymph vessels are creamy yellow. The nodes look like small peas.

OUR DIGESTIVE SYSTEM

►The digestion of the food we eat begins in the mouth. Saliva from the salivary glands contains chemicals which start to break food down into substances our body can absorb. The stomach and intestines complete this process.

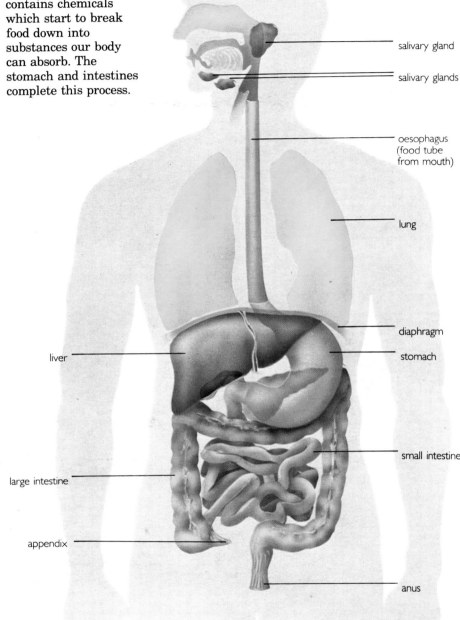

salivary gland

salivary glands

oesophagus (food tube from mouth)

lung

diaphragm

stomach

liver

small intestine

large intestine

appendix

anus

If you have a pain somewhere in the middle of your body, you may say 'my stomach hurts!' But what is hurting may not be your stomach at all. It could be some other part of the long tube which begins at one end with a hole in your face, the mouth. It goes through the body and ends with a hole in your bottom, the

anus. Along this tube food passes and is digested. This means it is slowly changed into a form that the body's cells can use.

The stomach

The stomach, the best known part of this tube, is a bag just under the diaphragm. It is lined with a special layer of cells. In one day (twenty-four hours) they pour into the stomach about three litres ($5\frac{1}{4}$ pints) of acid and other juices to act on the food. Some of these cells also produce a sticky liquid called *mucus*, that protects the stomach from the digestive juices. Without it, the acid juices would destroy the stomach's own cells. The muscles of the stomach contract and relax about three times a minute. This gentle motion churns up the food with the juices and soon it becomes a liquid.

Food does not stay in the stomach until it is completely digested. Depending on what sort of food it is, it moves down into the intestines, often very quickly. A mixture of different sorts of food, perhaps meat, potatoes and a green vegetable, could take about two hours to leave the stomach completely.

The intestines

The food continues to change as it moves along the long coil of our intestines. In the intestines the useful parts of the food are further broken down by special juices, and absorbed into the body, first water and then other nourishing substances. What the body cannot use goes into the large intestine and is eventually discarded.

The appendix

Attached to the top of the large intestine is a very mysterious little organ, the appendix. Even today no one is quite sure what it is meant to do. Some scientists think it is just a useless organ, left over in the body from a time, long long ago, when we ate very different kinds of food. Others think it may play some part in fighting disease within the body. We do know that sometimes it becomes very swollen and red (inflamed). When this happens, a person will have a very bad pain near the belly button or low on the right side. They will not want to eat and will vomit. When this happens, they must go into hospital quickly and the appendix will be cut out of the body at once.

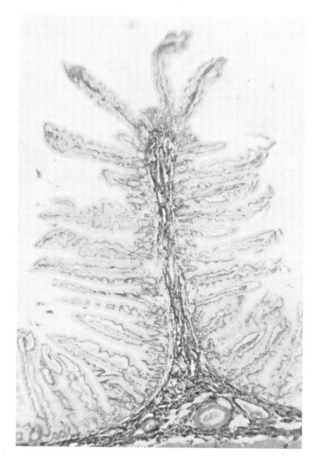

▲In the walls of the intestines there are thousands of little branched structures called villi. Here is one, photographed through a microscope and enlarged 50 times. You can see the cells very clearly.

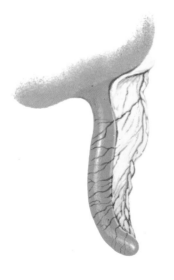

◄When an appendix becomes inflamed like this, it is very dangerous. It could actually burst inside the body and if this happened, a person could die. That is why appendicitis is always treated quickly.

OUR LIVER, KIDNEYS AND SPLEEN

The liver

Many organs that are constantly busy within us give no outside clues to what they are doing. The largest organ in the body, the liver, sits very quietly just below our ribs on the right side. It does not beat or move but it carries out more than five hundred tasks. So long as it is healthy we are not aware of what it is doing.

The liver deals with the chemicals our body has made from the food we eat. Some it stores until the cells need it. Others it works on itself, changing them into substances to be used at once. Sometimes the food we eat contains small amounts of poisons called toxins. The liver makes these harmless. It also breaks down old red blood cells. The liver removes the iron from them so it can be used to make new cells. Because the liver is always busy and its work so important it has a double blood supply.

The liver makes bile, its own special chemical. Bile is stored in a little sac called the gall bladder. From there it drips through a special opening, a duct, into the intestines. Bile helps the intestines change fatty, greasy foods into useful nourishment. Sometimes the bile duct becomes blocked. If the condition is very bad, a doctor may have to remove the gall bladder. After that a person will probably have to be careful about eating fatty foods. We can live without our gall bladder, but not without our liver.

The kidneys

Tucked carefully inside us at waistline level and protected by a thick overcoat of fat are the kidneys. Just as the lungs remove carbon dioxide from the blood and add oxygen to it, so the kidneys take out harmful substances and make sure that the amount of water is just right. The kidneys change water the body no longer needs into urine. The urine carries with it the other substances the kidneys have filtered out of the blood. Slowly urine collects in the bladder. When that bag becomes full, we know we must get rid of the urine.

If one kidney should be injured in some

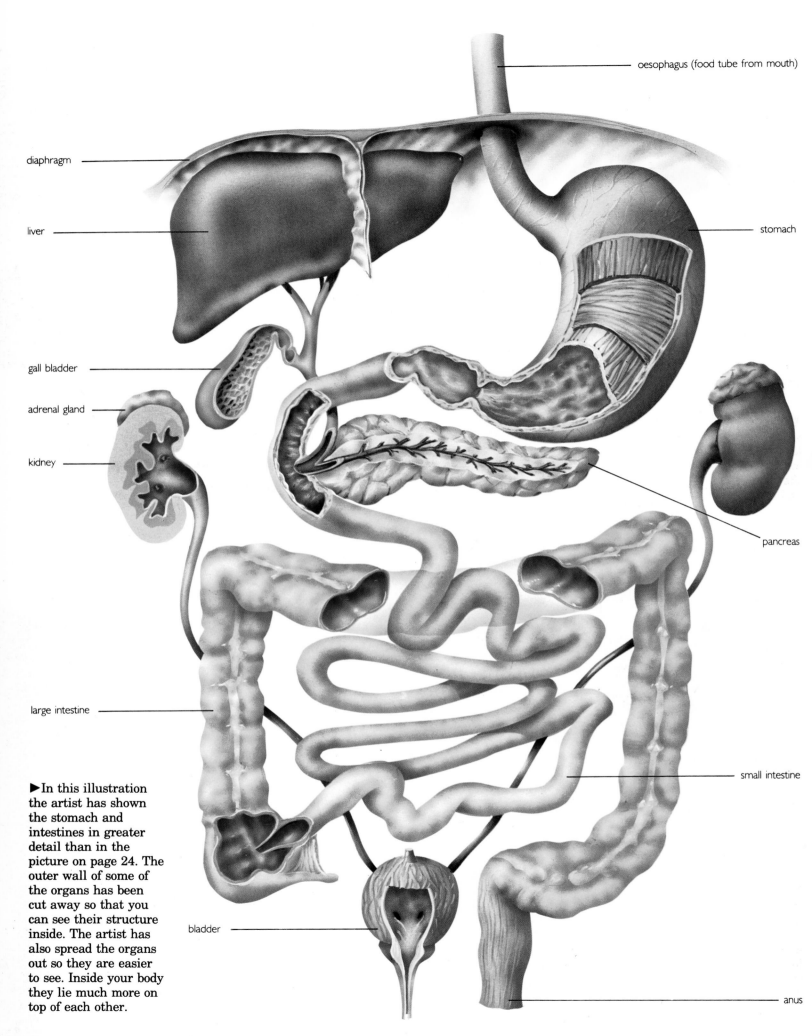

oesophagus (food tube from mouth)

diaphragm

liver

gall bladder

adrenal gland

kidney

stomach

pancreas

large intestine

small intestine

►In this illustration
the artist has shown
the stomach and
intestines in greater
detail than in the
picture on page 24. The
outer wall of some of
the organs has been
cut away so that you
can see their structure
inside. The artist has
also spread the organs
out so they are easier
to see. Inside your body
they lie much more on
top of each other.

bladder

anus

26

way, the remaining one can work hard enough to keep our blood healthy. If both fail, our blood must be purified regularly by a machine unless it is possible for doctors to put someone else's kidney (a transplant) into our body.

The spleen

The spleen is a small organ quite close to the liver and the stomach. It is useful to the body in an emergency because it can produce white blood cells to fight disease. It stores extra blood and can release it into the body when we need it quickly. Like the liver, it helps to break down old red blood cells. It also makes some special substances called *antibodies* which also fight disease. If the spleen is injured or removed from the body, other organs take over its work.

▼This drawing shows what a small part of the inside of the liver looks like. You can see the arteries (in red) and the veins (in blue).

The bile channels are small tubes carrying bile to the gall bladder and the liver cells make the bile and act on food.

◄In the **top** picture we see someone sleeping as his blood passes through a complicated machine, an artificial kidney, to be purified. This must be done every five days. On the **right** two doctors are putting a human kidney into a special machine to keep it healthy. It can be kept in the machine for 24 hours before being transplanted into another person.

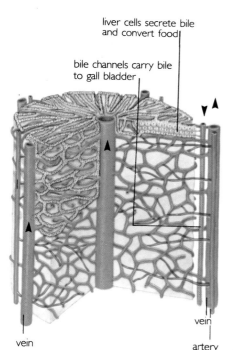

liver cells secrete bile and convert food

bile channels carry bile to gall bladder

vein

vein

artery

►These delicate curling hairs are really the thousands of collecting tubes inside a kidney. They are highly magnified and show us the way urine is gathered before it goes to the bladder.

GLANDS – MAKERS OF CHEMICALS

▶The pituitary gland at the base of the brain makes the growth hormone. This man is what is called a pituitary giant, because he has too much growth hormone. At 21 years old he was 2.3m (7ft 10in) and still had not stopped growing.

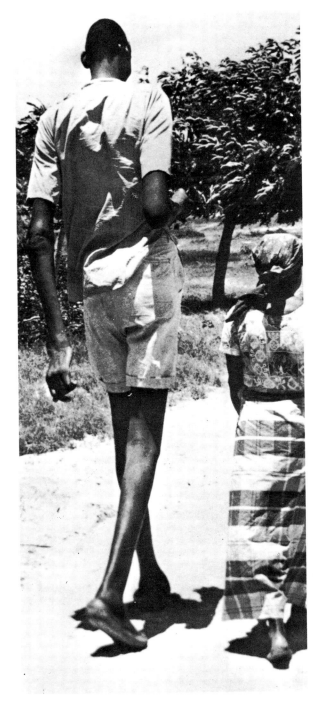

The work that the heart, lungs, stomach, or blood does is easy to understand. Other parts of the body are also very important to life, but what they do and how they do it is more difficult to see. Glands are like this. Doctors and scientists today are studying them a great deal. Each new bit of information seems to make them more and more important.

All over the body as well as deep within it there are special groups of cells making chemicals. Usually they form a little pocket. The chemical they make collects at the bottom. Some have small tubes called ducts to release the chemical into the blood. Others have no ducts but tiny blood vessels pass through the gland. The blood picks up the chemical, often called a hormone, as it passes through.

The work of some glands is easy to see. Sweat glands are just beneath our skin. When we are hot we see the moisture they release on to our skin to help us cool down. When we cry, our tears are a salty liquid produced by a gland in the corner of our eye. When a girl is fully grown, she has breasts. These are just large glands. When she has a baby, they produce milk to feed it.

The pituitary gland

The small glands within our bodies are very important. Deep in the centre of the brain is the pituitary gland. It makes some of the most important hormones in the body. It controls our blood pressure and the work of the kidneys. Its hormones, moving through the blood, tell the body just how fast it should grow. It gives the signal when a baby is ready to be born. Its chemicals act as triggers, setting most of the other glands to work.

Some other important glands

At the bottom of the throat the thyroid and parathyroid make hormones that affect how much energy we have. The thyroid can make us burn up the energy from food quickly. The parathyroid produces a hormone which acts on muscles and bones. On top of the kidneys, like two bubbly hats, are the adrenals.

▲In some diseases, for example jaundice, too much bile is produced by the liver. It makes the eyeball look yellow, as this picture shows.

They make among other things the well-known hormone, adrenalin. When we are really frightened or angry, adrenalin pours into our blood, releasing stored-up energy. This gives us strength to fight or run away. Just below the stomach is the pancreas, a gland that produces chemicals to help digest food and hormones. One is insulin, which controls the way the body uses sugar. Sometimes the pancreas does not make enough insulin. Then a person gets a disease called diabetes.

The sex glands

The best known glands are the sex glands. When she grows up, a girl's ovaries make the hormones which gradually change the shape of her body. They make it possible for her to have babies. In a boy, the testes produce hormones that change his shape, cause more hair to grow on his face and body. They make it possible for him to produce the seed necessary to start a baby.

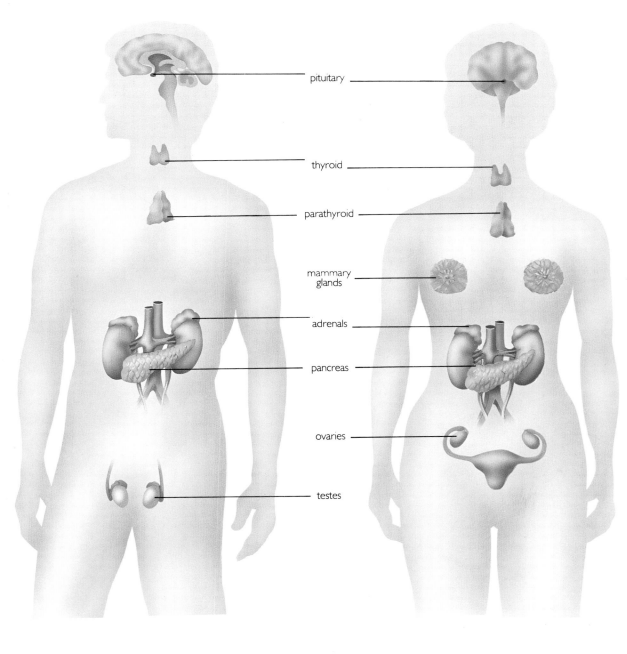

pituitary

thyroid

parathyroid

mammary glands

adrenals

pancreas

ovaries

testes

◀These major glands are often called endocrine glands. That word means ductless. The hormones they produce act as special messengers and they travel rapidly through the blood to reach their target organs.

MUSCLES AND THEIR WORK

►Here is a modern map of the main voluntary muscles in the body. Sometimes these are called skeletal muscles because they are attached to the skeleton and move the bones. Our muscles make up half our body weight. You may find it interesting to compare this drawing with the one made by Vesalius so many years ago, on page 10. As you can see, we still call muscles by the Latin names given to them when all scientists and doctors wrote only in Latin.

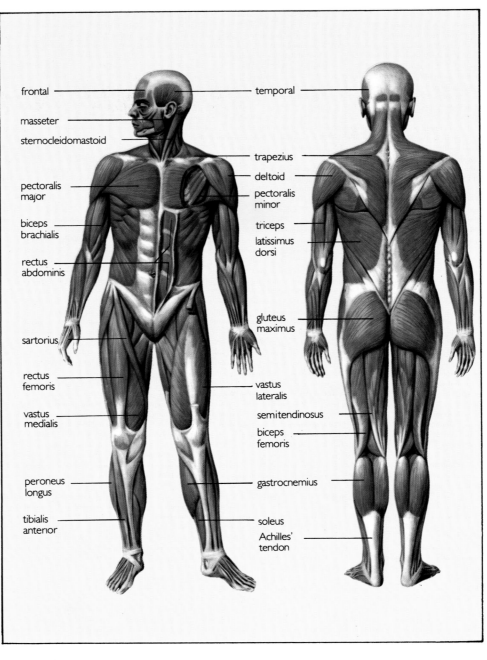

frontal — temporal
masseter
sternocleidomastoid — trapezius
— deltoid
pectoralis major — pectoralis minor
biceps brachialis — triceps
— latissimus dorsi
rectus abdominis
— gluteus maximus
sartorius
rectus femoris — vastus lateralis
vastus medialis — semitendinosus
— biceps femoris
peroneus longus — gastrocnemius
tibialis anterior — soleus
Achilles' tendon

▼Voluntary muscles can only pull, not push, so they always work in pairs. When the top extends, the bottom contracts. The drawing shows clearly how the long muscles in the thigh work to bend and straighten the leg.

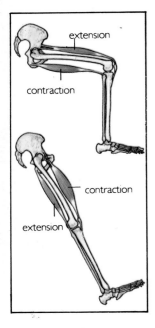

extension
contraction
contraction
extension

We all find out something about how our muscles work when we are very small. We try to lift or push something that is too heavy for us. We can feel something happening in our arms. We see bulges under the skin – our muscles at work. When we run and play for a long time, the backs of our legs sometimes start to hurt. The muscles there are signalling that they are tired.

Different kinds of muscle
There are hundreds of other muscles in the body, some so small they can be seen only under a microscope. We use muscles for every movement we make. Some movements we chose to do, like throwing a ball or biting an apple. The muscles we use then are called voluntary muscles.

Other movements we never think about but they happen all the same. Our stomach churns up the food we eat. The diaphragm pushes air in and out of our lungs. These are called involuntary muscles. Our brain directs them automatically. Involuntary muscles also open and close the many tubes inside the body. Most tubes have two layers of this sort of cell around them. One layer contracts (closes up) the tube and the other expands (widens or opens) it.

The heart is a kind of involuntary

cells   cross
                                         section

1
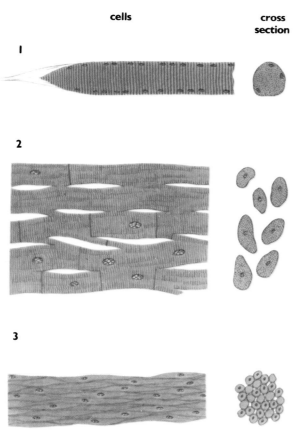

2

3

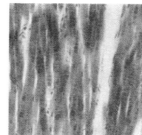

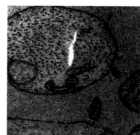

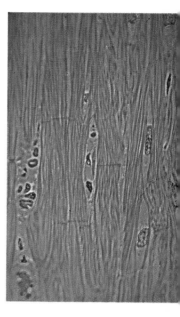

◄Drawings show us exactly how different each type of muscle cell is and we can then check this against a photograph of real muscle tissue taken through a microscope.
1 Voluntary or skeletal muscle has very long cells making strong fibres.
2 The heart (cardiac) muscle is made up of shorter fat cells that seem to make a network.
3 Involuntary muscle cells are narrow and look smoother. The dots are the nuclei of the cells.

▲This picture of heart (cardiac) muscle was taken through a microscope even more powerful than in picture 2. You can see the nuclei and the muscle's striped appearance very clearly.

muscle but it does its work on its own. It does not need any signals from the brain although the brain can sometimes instruct it to beat faster or slower.

Different kinds of muscle cell
Muscles are made of very special cells that are easy to recognise under a microscope. They look like narrow threads or fibres. They have more than one nucleus per cell. Some have thousands of nuclei per cell. Voluntary muscle cells are the most unusual of all, they seem to have stripes going across the fibres. Heart muscle cells are fatter than voluntary muscle cells. Involuntary muscle cells are narrower and smaller, they are smooth and not striped.

Voluntary muscles at work
Exercise can make voluntary muscles grow larger. You are not growing more muscles but the fibres of the ones you have get thicker and stronger. If you exercise too much or for too long, your muscles start to hurt. You may stumble or drop a ball. You begin to suffer what is called 'fatigue'. What has happened is

that the hard working muscle cells have been using up food and oxygen very fast. As this 'burns up' within the cell, the cell throws off water and carbon dioxide as waste. The body needs time to get rid of this. When you are rested and the muscles cleared of waste, you can exercise hard again.

▼Exercise and training makes muscles strong, but you do not need muscles like these two men – unless you compete in body-building contests.

OUR NERVOUS SYSTEM

▼The spinal cord is connected to the brain. Messages from the brain travel down the spinal cord and along the motor nerves to muscles. Messages from the sense organs travel along the sensory nerves. The axons send messages and the dendrites pick up messages from the cells.

Blood goes into every part of our body and carries hormones, the chemical messages, to the cells. We have another communication system as well. Like a huge computer network, it is constantly sending and receiving messages. It uses tiny bursts of electricity as well as chemicals. This is the nervous system and its main control centre is the brain.

Sending messages through the body

Nerve cells, called neurones, are specially built so they can receive and send messages. Around the cell body are little branches called dendrites. These pick up messages from other cells. One branch is much longer than the others. This is the axon and sends messages. If the neurone is a motor cell, one that works a muscle, it could have an axon over a meter (39.37 inches) long. Inside the brain though there are millions of neurones so small they can be seen only with very powerful electron microscopes.

When a lot of axons are bunched together, as in arms and legs, they look like long white strings. Each axon has a covering called the myelin sheath. This

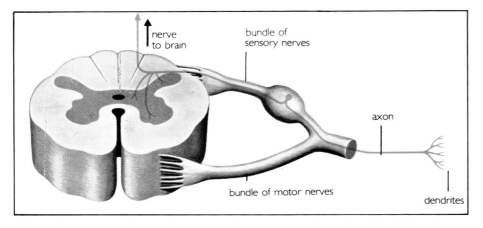

▼The dark patches in this picture are cell bodies of neurones in the brain. The thin threads are dendrites and the thick threads axons. There are billions of cells like this in the brain.

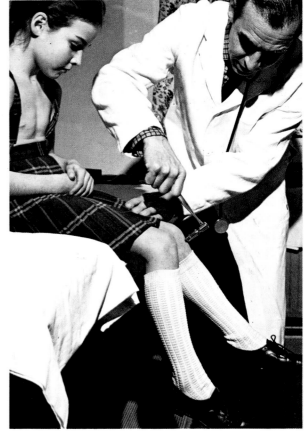

▼Some of our actions are very fast and we do not think about them at all. They are called reflexes. If a doctor taps just below the knee (**above**) the bottom part of the leg will jerk up at once. If he runs something from the heel to the toes on the bottom of a child's foot, the toes will curl (**above left**). These reflexes happen because the nerves use a special switching system within the spinal cord and the information does not have to go all the way to the brain and back.

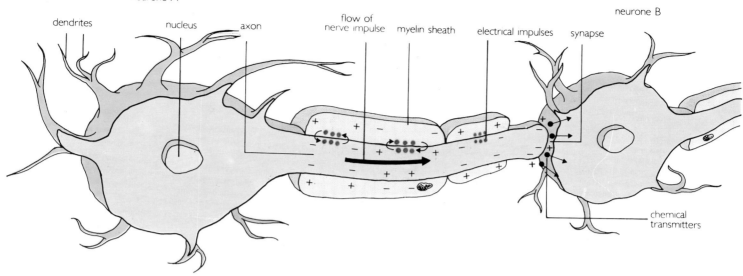

neurone A

dendrites   nucleus   axon

flow of
nerve impulse   myelin sheath   electrical impulses   synapse

neurone B

chemical
transmitters

works very much like the covering on electrical wires. It protects the axon and makes the electrical signals travel faster. There is a tiny gap between the tip of one axon and another in the linking chain. That gap is called a synapse. To cross the gap, a message from the brain triggers chemicals that shoot from one axon to another. On reaching the new axon, the message becomes electrical again and proceeds further. All the messages go in one direction only. Another line of neurones send messages back to the brain. This keeps the signals separate.

Because the system is so complex, it takes time for messages to go from the brain to other parts of our body. Neurones working for our eyes pick up a message about what we see, our brain sorts it and then sends out other messages to make our legs move us out of danger quickly. This is called 'reaction time' and can be as little as the tiniest fraction of a second. Some people have much faster reaction times than others.

Like our system of muscles, a whole group of nerves act automatically, without us thinking about them. They are the nerves sending messages to many of the involuntary muscles in organs like our lungs, stomach, intestines and bladder. There are also special neurones which pick up messages from all our senses. They tell us what we are hearing, seeing, touching and tasting. Another group of nerves acts very closely with all our glands and these are the nerves that influence our feelings and moods.

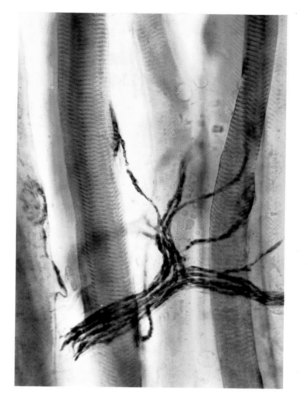

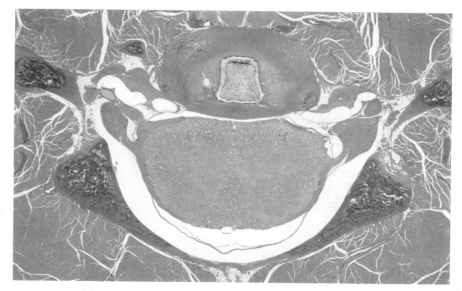

▲This drawing gives a good idea of how information travels from neurone A to neurone B. We see how the electrical impulses become chemical at the synapse and then change back and continue their journey in the new cell.

◄This highly magnified photograph from a microscope shows axons connecting with muscle fibres.

▼The bones (vertebrae) of the backbone protect the spinal cord. The large central area in the picture is the spinal cord, the darker areas around it a vertebra.

THE BRAIN AND ITS WORK

Inside our head, well protected by the strong bones of the skull, is the most important organ of the body, the brain. Clever doctors and wonderful machines can keep us alive for a time if our lungs stop working or our heart stops beating. If our brain stops working, nothing can be done. We are dead.

How the brain works

Day and night, billions of neurones in the brain are sending out and receiving tiny electrical messages. They are also storing, in a way we do not yet understand, information and memories. When we are awake, the brain sorts information from the senses, particularly our eyes. We then act on the information. Although many animals can see farther and more sharply than us they cannot make use of all the information their eyes provide. Animals do not have 'association fibres' in their brains. These are special nerve links from one part of the brain to the other. These make it possible for us to link up and understand what we see. Animal brains also do not have a language centre, a place that makes it possible for us to use thousands of words instead of just a few sounds. Our language centre makes us

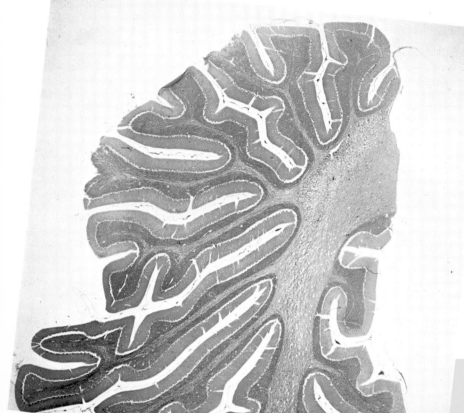

▲Here is a small piece of the part of the brain which coordinates movements like walking. The light orange areas are cells that actually do the work, the darker area is protective tissue.

►By cutting away part of the cerebrum, the artist gives us a chance to see into the brain. All the parts are linked by millions and millions of neurons. From the medulla oblongata nerve fibres go down into the spinal cord and through it to the rest of the body.

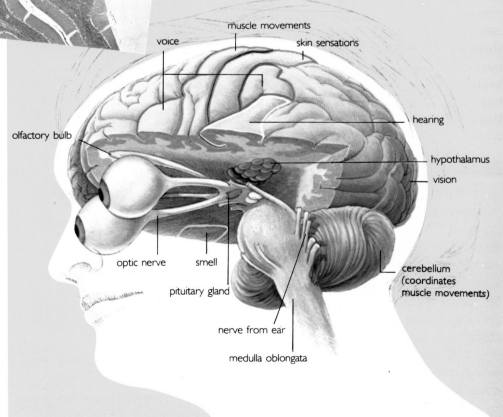

muscle movements

voice

skin sensations

olfactory bulb

hearing

hypothalamus

vision

optic nerve

smell

cerebellum (coordinates muscle movements)

pituitary gland

nerve from ear

medulla oblongata

able to speak and understand what people say to us.

Even while we sleep the brain is busy. The medulla oblongata, a part at the base of the brain, keeps all our automatic body systems, such as breathing and digesting food, working smoothly. Other centres in the brain work while we sleep. They control what and how long we dream. Generally, though, the electrical signals coming from our brain while we sleep are more simple and slow.

How the brain is made

When we look at a picture of a human brain we see a crumpled grey jelly divided into two halves like a walnut. We are looking at the cerebrum, the envelope layer that contains all the centres dealing with movement and the senses. Within the brain are the thalamus and hypothalamus. One is the main relay station for the body's internal messages and the other controls hunger, thirst, how warm or cold we feel, and some other emotions. The olfactory bulb brings in information about smells. The optic nerve carries information from the eyes. Safe in the centre of the brain is the pituitary gland. Curiously, if the right half or hemisphere of the brain is slightly larger than the left, a person will be left-handed. If the left side is bigger, the person will be right-handed. All the nerves from each side cross over neatly at the base of the skull. No one yet knows why.

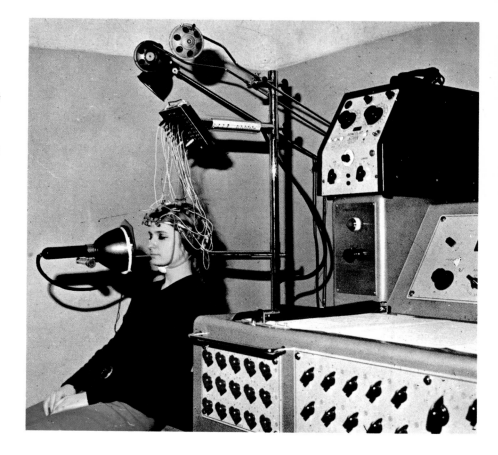

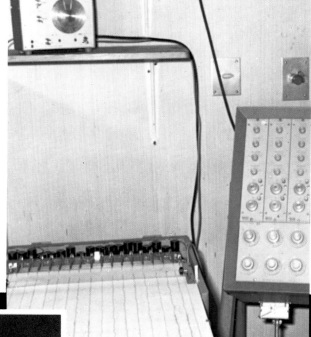

▲The girl above has wires attached to her head to pick up the tiny electric bursts her brain cells are making. Where the wires are attached will give the scientists information about which part of the brain is working. On the left we see the machine that is taking down the information coming from the girl's brain. The automatic pencil is recording the electrical brain waves from her brain. This is an absolutely painless procedure.

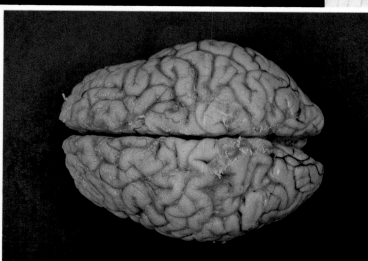

◄Photograph of the human brain taken from above. The crumpled look of the brain's surface shows very clearly.

HOW WE SEE

Most of the information about the world we live in comes to us through our eyes. We see colour, size, shape, texture, and movement. We recognise food and avoid harmful things. We know the faces of our family and friends. We can find our way from place to place. Although we also learn through hearing, touch and taste, we learn most through our eyes.

The human eye is like a round camera tucked into a special protective opening in the skull. It works by using light as it bounces off all the objects around us.

Without light we cannot see. Even on a very dark night there is some light. That is why we can see dim shapes. Light comes into the eye through the black hole in the centre, the pupil. Sometimes a person's pupils may seem much larger than usual. This is because our pupils expand to let more light into the eye when light is poor. Animals' eyes do the same thing. Notice how different the eyes of a cat or dog look when they come in from the night.

As light passes through the eye it is collected (focussed) by a special strip of transparent tissue, the lens. If it is healthy the lens will focus the light on to a screen of special cells, the retina, at the back of the eyeball. There, cells called rods and cones because of their shape, will sort out all the parts of the light that make a single image, its colour, size and movement. They translate this information into tiny bursts of electricity that move along the optic nerve to the brain. The brain makes sense of what we see.

Helping our eyes
Sometimes the lenses in a person's eyes do not make a clear image on the retina or they focus the image on the wrong place. Man-made lenses of specially curved glass worn in front of the eye help the lenses in the eye with their work. Today millions of people wear contact lenses, tiny lenses of plastic that float on the surface of the eye. These lenses, like glasses, help the natural lenses within the eye to focus images correctly. When they are well fitted they are usually so comfortable a person forgets they are there. But contact lenses must be taken out when a person sleeps and they must be treated with great care.

The body has many ways of protecting our eyes. We blink, close our eyes instantly, if something comes too close to the eye or wind blows into them. Tears will come to our eyes at once if something harmful falls into them. Even our eyelashes are important. They catch little specks of dust and dirt before they can reach the eyes.

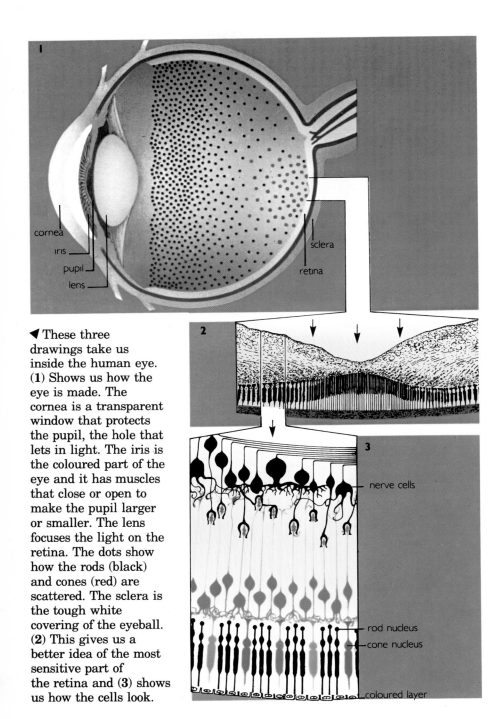

◀ These three drawings take us inside the human eye. (**1**) Shows us how the eye is made. The cornea is a transparent window that protects the pupil, the hole that lets in light. The iris is the coloured part of the eye and it has muscles that close or open to make the pupil larger or smaller. The lens focuses the light on the retina. The dots show how the rods (black) and cones (red) are scattered. The sclera is the tough white covering of the eyeball. (**2**) This gives us a better idea of the most sensitive part of the retina and (**3**) shows us how the cells look.

cornea
iris
pupil
lens
sclera
retina
nerve cells
rod nucleus
cone nucleus
coloured layer

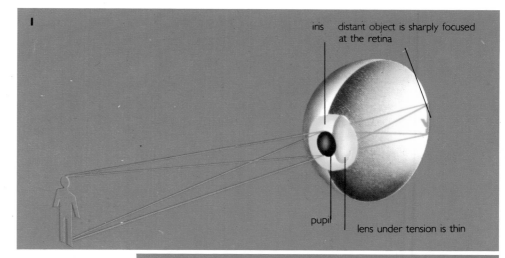

1

iris   distant object is sharply focused
        at the retina

pupil   lens under tension is thin

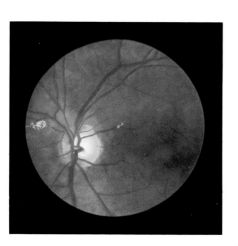

◄If we look into the eye with a special machine, the retina looks like a red disc. The yellow spot is the blind spot in the eye where the nerves come together.

►How our eyes focus. When the lens is under tension, a sharp image of a distant object is focused on the retina (1). (The image is upside down, but the brain makes it seem the right way round.) With the lens still under tension (2) a near object appears blurred. When the lens is relaxed (3) a near object is sharply focused, while a distant object (4) is blurred.

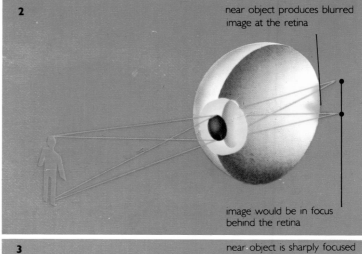

2

near object produces blurred image at the retina

image would be in focus behind the retina

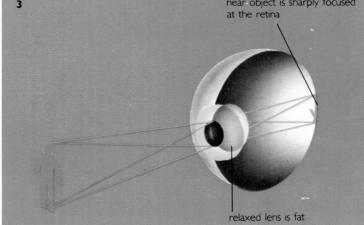

3

near object is sharply focused at the retina

relaxed lens is fat

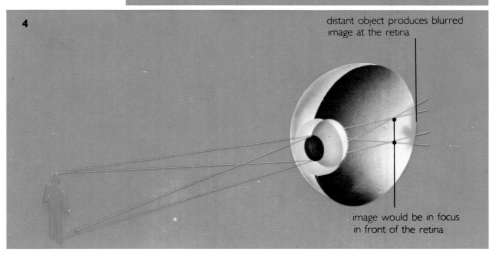

4

distant object produces blurred image at the retina

image would be in focus in front of the retina

HOW WE HEAR

We may think we hear with our ears, those cupped shapes of tissue on either side of our head, but that is not the whole truth. The part of the ear we see is just the starting point. The outer ear collects sound and funnels it into the ear passage to the middle and inner parts of the ear. Across the tube of the middle ear is stretched a delicate membrane, the eardrum. When sound reaches it, it shakes. How quickly and strongly it shakes depends on whether the sound is high or low, loud or soft. This movement or vibration from the eardrum then passes along a chain of tiny delicate bones and at the end there is another membrane, the oval window. Beyond the oval window is the inner ear. Here all the vibrations of membranes and bones are changed into electrical impulses. They, in turn, travel along nerves to reach a special centre in the brain. That is how we hear and understand the sound around us.

Keeping our balance

The inner ear has another important job – it gives us our sense of balance which we need to stand and move. Within the inner ear are semi-circular canals filled with fluid and containing thousands of tiny hairs. When we move our head, even very slightly, the fluid moves too, the hairs pick up the signal and a message

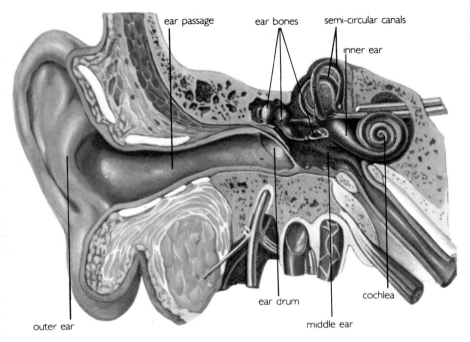

ear passage · ear bones · semi-circular canals · inner ear · ear drum · cochlea · middle ear · outer ear

▲The drawing shows the whole ear: outer, middle and inner. We can see the way sound must travel to reach deep into the head and we can see how close the semicircular canals and the cochlea are.

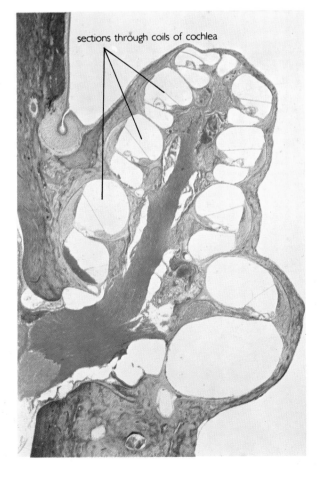

sections through coils of cochlea

►The cochlea, part of the inner ear, is the place where the tiny hairs on the basilar membrane pick up sound. A slice through it seen under a microscope shows the way the tubes curl.

▼A quick and simple test with a tuning fork can tell a doctor if a patient is deaf or not.

goes to the brain. Then, if necessary, we can change our position.

Other kinds of ear

Most creatures have hearing organs of some sort, although they may look very different from human ears. Some, like elephants, have large flaps to collect sound more easily to warn against enemies. Others, bats for example, can hear sounds which humans miss. Even under water, sea creatures have hearing organs to help them avoid danger and locate food.

▶Whales have keen hearing because it is difficult to see in deep water. They use sound to communicate with each other and to hunt.

◀ A bat has good hearing because it hunts in poor light. It makes very high sounds itself and can hear them bouncing off surfaces.

◀A rabbit depends on its very good hearing to protect it from its many enemies.

◀An African elephant is on the alert, his ears pointed toward a possible source of danger. The big ear flaps will pick up the sound.

◀A grasshopper hears with a simple membrane that vibrates like our eardrums.

39

HOW WE SPEAK

Air moving in and out of our nose, mouth and lungs does more than give oxygen to our cells and take away carbon dioxide. Working with our teeth, tongue, mouth and special tissue in our throat, it makes talking possible. When we speak, air coming from our lungs passes across small flaps of tissue at the back of our throat. These are just behind the bulge we often call the voice box or Adam's apple. Its correct name is the larynx. The flaps are vocal cords. They make the moving air shake rapidly or vibrate. All sound is air vibrating in some special way, fast or slow, strong or weak.

What sort of sound we make depends on how the cords are stretched. The strings of a guitar or any similar musical instrument work the same way. But we need more than vocal cords to speak. The empty places in our mouth and nose act just like the wooden parts of a violin, cello, guitar, or harp. They shape the sound and make it louder. Children's voices are high and lighter than the voices of adults because their vocal cords are thinner and shorter and the open spaces in their head smaller. As we grow our larynx grows like the rest of us. A boy's larynx grows bigger than a girl's. His vocal cords become longer and thicker. This is why a man has a deeper voice than a woman.

Speech and language

The lips, tongue, roof of the mouth and jaws all work with the vocal cords to produce speech. Together they are called the vocal tract. Speech sounds have two groups, vowels and consonants. These are the building blocks of all languages. Vowel sounds are the broad, smooth sounds we make when we cut the flow of air into small bursts using our tongue, lips and teeth. Some African languages have special sounds called clicks, but they too use vowels and consonants for the main parts of their words.

Scientists have not yet discovered exactly how we learn to speak. Babies certainly learn much by imitating what they hear. Some very bright animals like chimpanzees and dolphins can be taught to understand and use signals to express simple ideas. Parrots and a few other birds can imitate the human voice saying a word or two. No bird or animal can use speech like a human being.

▶If we look down into the throat we can see exactly where the sound of the voice is produced. When we say something the vocal cords vibrate to make the sounds. The epiglottis, a flap of tough tissue at the back of the throat, makes sure that when we swallow, air, not food, is all that goes down the windpipe into the lungs.

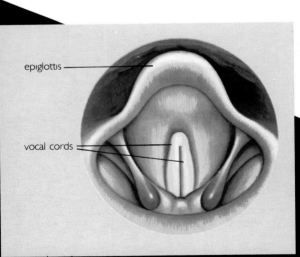

epiglottis

vocal cords

nose cavity

roof of mouth

tongue
epiglottis

vocal cords

windpipe

spine

▲When we see how much space there is for sound to move in inside our head it is easy to understand how we can make so many words and different sounds when we sing.

◀Dolphins are apparently very intelligent. They can learn tricks and we know that they have a 'language' and can communicate with each other.

◄These deaf children are learning sign language so that they can communicate with each other. We need to hear what we are saying in order to learn to speak properly. Deaf children can be taught to speak by feeling with their hands the vibrations different sounds make in their throats and the different way air comes out of their mouths when they say different words.

►Although parrots and macaws can imitate some human sounds, they cannot 'talk' because their voice box is quite different.

SMELLING AND TASTING

Smell and taste are two senses that work together closely. Sometimes we can be mistaken about which one is supplying us with the information. If you have a bad cold and your nose is blocked you will find your food tastes flat and dull. You may even say 'I've lost my sense of taste'. This is not true. The smell of food sends messages to the brain very quickly and those messages are added to ones coming from the mouth. Together they make up flavour or taste.

Our nose
The human nose is divided into two passages inside. Each, in turn, has three smaller parts. They all have a thick lining of cells that make the sticky fluid, mucus. When the lining is irritated it produces too much mucus. Then we must blow our nose and sometimes the passages feel blocked and painful. The lining of the nose contains many tiny blood vessels. Their job is to warm the air on its way to our lungs but if we bump our nose, they may bleed. At the very top of the inside of the nose the mucus membrane contains many special cells that end in tiny hairs. These hairs catch the invisible bits of chemicals called *molecules* that float in the air. Molecules are far smaller than the tiniest cell. Everything has molecules in it and certain molecules belong to certain smells. When the hairs catch the molecule they can send information about it directly into the brain.

Our tongue
Taste, too, works by special cells detecting messages from molecules, this time in food or drink and not in the air. Our tongue is covered by 9,000 tiny bumps, the taste buds. Most are on the top of the tongue and each part of the tongue deals with a different sort of taste. We notice whichever is the strongest. Coffee and tea are naturally bitter but sugar will make them seem sweet.

Sometimes the taste buds cannot send messages to the brain. If we eat something that is very hot or very cold, they stop working for a time and all we taste is 'hotness' or 'coldness'. If we keep the same food in the mouth for a long time, the taste buds stop sending messages to the brain about it.

►The taste buds are arranged to pick up information on the four main flavour groups: bitter, sour, salt and sweet. Everything we taste is a combination of these with a particular smell.

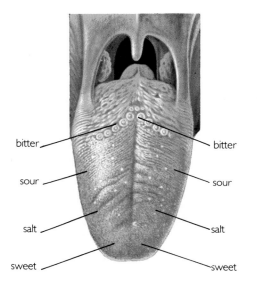

bitter — bitter
sour — sour
salt — salt
sweet — sweet

►A drawing gives us a look inside a taste bud. The tiny hairlets pick up chemical molecules from the food through an opening, a pore. They pass information to the sensory cell. The nerve fibrils carry it further on its journey to the brain.

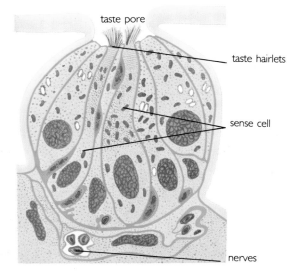

taste pore

taste hairlets

sense cell

nerves

▼The inside of your nose would look like this if it was as highly magnified as this picture. The hairs lining your nose collect information about smells. But not all hairs take information about all smells. Each group of hairs has a special cell to take its messages to the brain.

►These two men belong to one of the great champagne-making families of France. They are in the tasting room at the firm's main vineyards, trying samples of wine from different years and different vineyards. The success of their company depends on their highly developed senses of taste and smell.

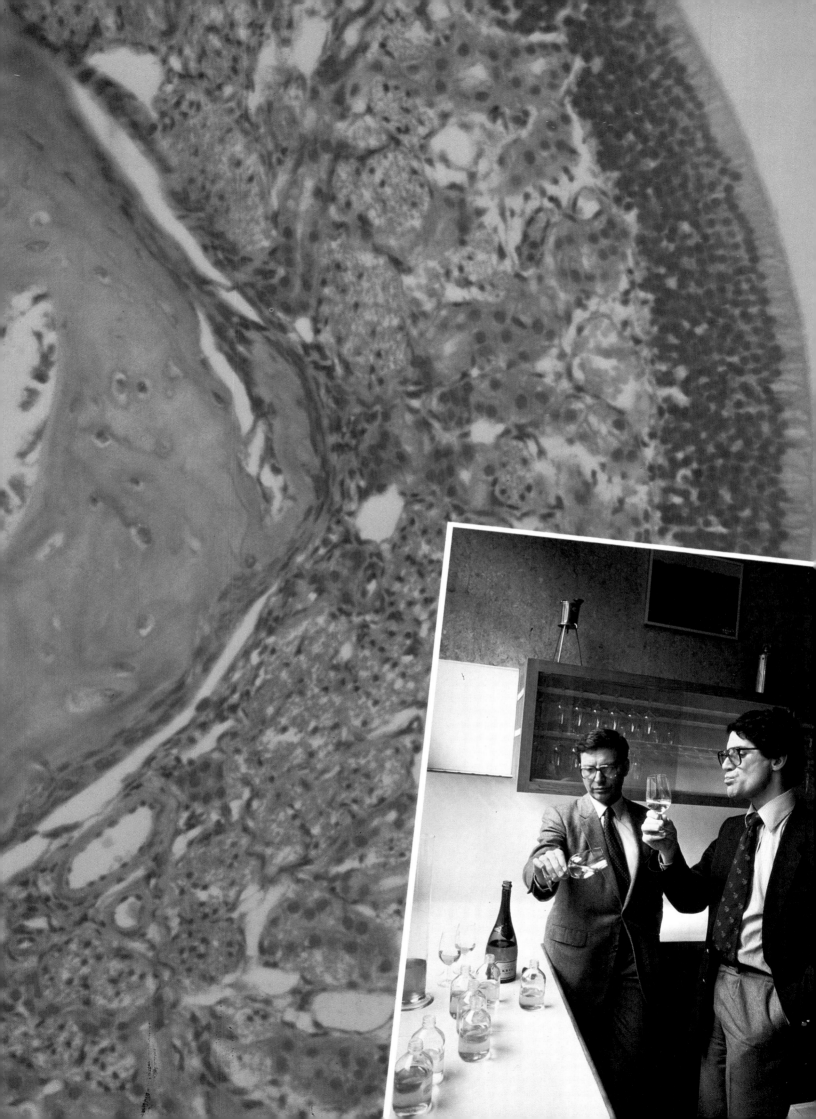

HOW WE MOVE

▲A baby learning to walk needs some help and encouragement. Slowly it learns to coordinate information from its eyes to judge distance while using its muscles in its arms and legs. Soon this becomes so easy the baby does not have to think to do it.

By now you probably understand why people often say the human body is a 'wonderful machine'. It certainly has thousands of moving parts, some so small they can be seen only with very powerful microscopes. Every moving part is controlled by muscles. To make these movements, each muscle has to work at the right moment. But muscles, except for the heart, do not work by themselves. They must have instructions from the nerves and the nerves get their instructions from the brain. The brain decides what instructions to give the muscles only after it has received messages from our senses: sight, hearing, touch, and sometimes taste and smell. If it is sending a message to muscles controlling the processes we do not usually think about, like breathing, it will have taken in other sorts of information from within our body and sent out the necessary messages.

We learn to coordinate – that is, make work together – our senses and our muscles when we are babies. A baby will see a brightly coloured toy. The message from his eye will go to his brain. The brain will make all the muscles in his arm and hand reach for the toy. Perhaps at first his chubby fingers will find it hard to grab what he wants but he will

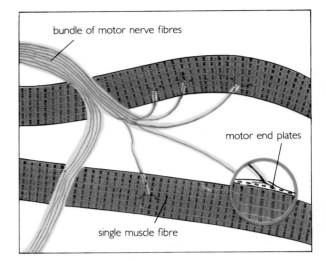

bundle of motor nerve fibres

motor end plates

single muscle fibre

▲Messages travel from the brain to the muscle fibres (brown) via the motor nerves (yellow) attached to the motor end plates. Nerve pulses cause the muscle fibres to contract.

▼Some people have better coordination than others. But no one could perform this kind of juggling feat without a long training and a great deal of practice.

▶A sport like judo is a test for the way the body moves and how fast messages from the brain can get to the limbs. Size and strength of body are not as important as coordination and speed.

practice until he can do this easily. We learn to walk in the same way, so moving is a combination of built-in features and learned skills.

Because so many parts of the body and brain must work together to make it possible for us to walk, run, eat, or play a game, there are many places where the system can break down. If an important nerve in our spine is cut our legs would stop receiving messages from the brain and we could not walk. If some disease hurts the muscles of our body they will not answer the brain's commands. Some people like sports stars and dancers seem to be able to move more smoothly or run faster and jump further than other

people. This usually is because they have been born with a good link between their muscles and brain and they have made it even better with practice.

◀ Playing any sport encourages concentration and develops coordination, but such internationally famous sportsmen as Vitas Gerulaitis (**left**) and Jimmy Connors (**below**) have developed both to a very high degree. The ace serves and amazing returns that thrill us in tennis matches would be impossible without superb coordination and swift reaction. Muscles are helpful too, but compare the arm muscles in these pictures with those of the body-builders on page 31.

SKIN – THE BODY'S ENVELOPE

▶A picture magnified many times shows a tube of epidermis going down into the dermis to make a follicle. The hair grows from the round base at the bottom. A small gland attached to the hair makes a greasy substance to protect it.

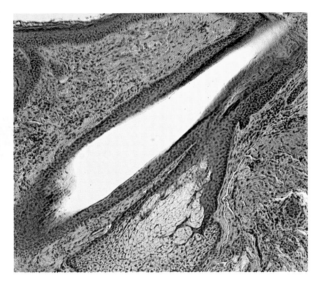

◀ A drawing of skin shows that it has two very different parts. The epidermis is made of about 20 layers of flat dead cells. New cells constantly grow at the bottom of the pile and slowly push their way to the top to replace cells flaking off. The dermis contains the blood vessels that feed the skin, as well as nerves, muscles and channels called ducts. Sweat or oil move through these to the surface. Hairs grow out to the surface through shafts called follicles.

Skin is a marvellous envelope that encloses the body. When we are hot, the blood vessels in it grow large, giving the blood a chance to cool. Sweat pours out to make the surface damp. When we are cold, the blood vessels grow small to hold heat within the body. Tips of nerve cells in the skin carry messages to the brain. We feel their effect when we touch things. Skin is completely waterproof and keeps out harmful substances. It can even

protect us from the effects of too much sunlight. Its cells, given enough time, can make a brown substance called melanin to give us a healthy tan instead of a dangerous burn.

The surface of the skin, the epidermis, contains a protein called keratin. Hair and nails are made up almost entirely of keratin. The dermis, which is thicker than the epidermis, looks like a network of tiny threads. Some are very rigid fibres called collagen and give the skin shape and texture. These fibres work less well as we age and that is why old people's skin sags and wrinkles.

Different creatures, different skins
Animals, fish, frogs, toads, snakes and birds all have different types of skin, suited to the way they live. Sharks have a rough, tough skin with sharp scales. Frogs have a moist skin to help them cope with living both on land and in the water. Birds have a very dry, loose skin which produces feathers. Their beaks and claws are made from keratin just like our hair and nails.

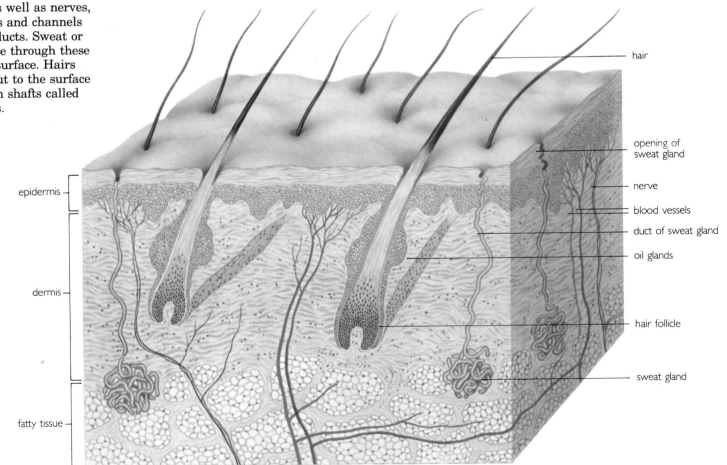

epidermis

dermis

fatty tissue

hair

opening of sweat gland

nerve

blood vessels

duct of sweat gland

oil glands

hair follicle

sweat gland

▲Birds have dry, loose skins which produce feathers. In contrast to the hammerhead stork, the hippo has immensely thick skin.

►The squirrel's claws are made of keratin, just like our nails and the stork's beak and claws.

RESPIRATION – ENERGY FROM THE AIR

►As we breathe, the strong dome of muscle, the diaphragm, pushes up or relaxes causing the lungs to draw in or expel air.

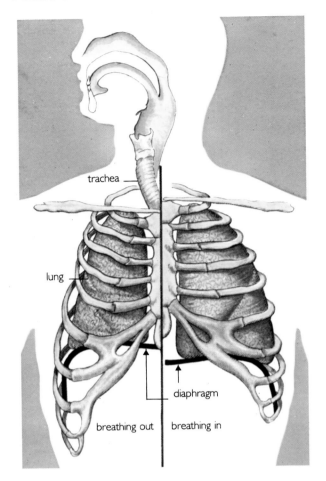

trachea

lung

diaphragm

breathing out | breathing in

As we discover what different parts of the body do and how they link up under the brain's control, we are learning about the systems that keep us alive. Many of these are similar to those in animals, and sometimes even in plants, but there are often interesting differences. The blood, heart, lungs, part of the nervous system and the brain work together so we can breathe. We need to breathe because our cells, like all other living cells, need energy to do their work. An important part of this energy comes from oxygen. The way a molecule of oxygen passes through a cell membrane and is exchanged for an unwanted molecule of carbon dioxide is called *respiration*. All the organs that help this process in the body make up the respiratory system.

When we watch a fish in a tank, we see its sides moving in and out like ours. Little bubbles of air move from its mouth to the surface of the water. The fish is breathing too, but it is taking in water, not air. There is a lot of oxygen in water too. The fish gulp water, forcing it back across the gills. The gills remove the oxygen from the water and then after it has been exchanged in the fish's lungs for carbon dioxide, used water and carbon dioxide go back into the sea. Because frogs spend part of their life on land and part in the water they are called amphibians. When they live in the water as tadpoles, they breathe through gills like a fish. As adults on land they take in oxygen through their moist skins, through blood vessels in the roof of their mouths and through lungs that work much like ours. Within their cells the same sort of respiratory process goes on.

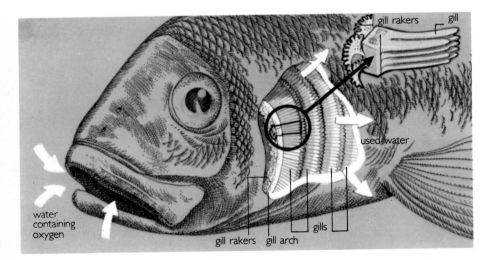

gill rakers | gill

used water

water containing oxygen

gill rakers | gill arch | gills

▲A fish swallows water constantly to breathe. The gill arch and gill rakers move the water along as the oxygen is removed from it.

◄A frog gets its oxygen in three ways but its blood carries it to all parts of its body just as ours does. A frog on dry land gulps air through its mouth. When it was a tadpole it could stay under water, taking air through its gills, like a fish.

►This plastic model shows how the blood vessels in our lungs branch like a tree. The bright red vessels carry blood with oxygen to the cells, the blue vessels carry blood with waste products that have been removed.

▼A man's lungs cannot remove oxygen from water the way fish can with their gills, so when he is underwater he takes air with him in a tank.

DIGESTION – ENERGY FROM FOOD

► In some countries there is not enough food. Children often do not have enough to eat and the little they have is not well balanced. Starving children often have swollen bellies. This is because their liver is full of fat and their digestive system is full of gas not food.

▼In other countries food is plentiful. There people often become ill because they eat too much or because they eat the wrong things.

Because our cells need food as well as oxygen to keep alive, a long chain of organs, beginning with our mouth and ending at the anus, make up our digestive system. This system too is controlled by the brain. Part of it functions automatically and part of it functions when we decide to take in more food. The brain also lets us know when we need more food or water by sending out signals of hunger or thirst. Sometimes the brain may send out the wrong signals and we eat far more than we need to do. Sometimes we may eat or drink for reasons which have nothing to

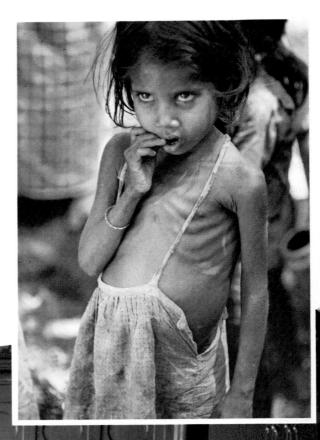

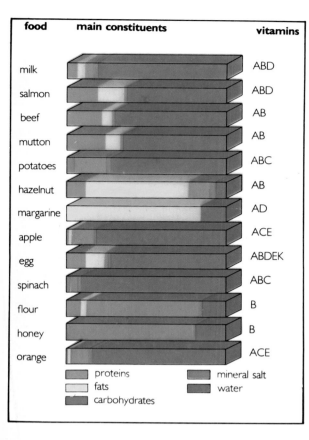

food	main constituents	vitamins
milk		ABD
salmon		ABD
beef		AB
mutton		AB
potatoes		ABC
hazelnut		AB
margarine		AD
apple		ACE
egg		ABDEK
spinach		ABC
flour		B
honey		B
orange		ACE

- proteins
- fats
- carbohydrates
- mineral salt
- water

◄The composition of some foods compared, together with their main vitamins. Minerals are only a small proportion of food, but then we need very small amounts, compared with protein, carbohydrate and fat. Honey, like candy, is mostly carbohydrate.

►Protein is the most expensive food, so scientists do a great deal of research into ways of producing nourishing protein cheaply, so that there will be enough for everyone. This research worker is experimenting with ways of growing small organisms, rich in protein, which can then be made into food.

do with our body needing the food. We may eat a piece of chocolate because we are bored. We may drink some coffee with a friend because we want to talk, not because we are thirsty.

Different kinds of food

All food we eat can be divided into three groups: *carbohydrates, fats* and *proteins*. In each part of the digestive system there are chemicals called enzymes which can work on one of these groups and help change it into a form the cells can use. Carbohydrates come from foods like bread and sugar. They give the body a form of energy that can be stored. If we take in too much, it turns into fat. Fats help make some body cells and also provide some energy, but they can make us put on weight if we take in too much. Proteins are the building materials of the body. We need them to make new cells. Muscles, hair, nails and skin are proteins. Many of the chemicals working inside our bodies are proteins. Milk, meat, fish, peas and beans are just some foods that are rich in proteins.

What about vitamins and minerals? They are mentioned on the labels of many foods we eat, breakfast cereals,

bread, snacks, even fruit juices. We are always told they are very important and we must have enough of them. They are really just substances that act as triggers for chemical activity within the body. We do need them but usually only in very small amounts. Vitamins were given alphabetical names, in the order in which they were discovered. Vitamin A was discovered before Vitamin D. Minerals are also needed in small amounts. Calcium, which is found in milk, is an important one, which we need for healthy bones, teeth, muscles and blood. An adult needs less than 0.8 of a gram a day, although a growing child needs more.

No single food can provide all the things the body needs to build new cells, make enough energy for life, and stay healthy. Eating too much of a single food can sometimes make you very ill. Carrots are a good vegetable to eat because they are rich in Vitamin A which keeps our eyes healthy. Too much Vitamin A is poisonous so eating nothing but carrots would be very unwise. Leaving out a major group of foods, like proteins, would also soon cause illness. A good diet is balanced, with all groups represented to meet the body's needs.

GROWING UP AND HAVING BABIES

As living things grow, they develop the ability to make more things like themselves. Some simple tiny creatures that live only a short time just split in half and each half becomes a new individual. Other creatures, and this includes human beings, take a long time to finish growing. When they reproduce, they can do so only sexually. That means a *male* cell has to join to a *female* cell to produce a new individual. In human beings, the male cell is called a sperm and the female cell, an ovum or egg. Sperms are made in a man's sex glands, the testes, which are clearly visible outside his body. Eggs are made in a woman's ovaries and they are tucked deep inside her body.

Human sex glands do not start to make cells that could begin a baby for a long time. When they do begin varies a great deal between individuals. Difference is caused by climate, where you live, and what food you eat. The changes can happen, and take several years to complete, any time between nine and seventeen years of age.

In boys, hair begins to grow under the armpits, between the legs and on the face as well. The voice becomes deeper. The penis, the tube that carries urine out of the body, becomes thicker and larger. Eventually it will be able to put a sperm into a woman's body to start a baby.

Girls gradually grow hair on their body too, but not their face. They start to have

▶As we grow up our bodies change a good deal, particularly between the ages of nine and seventeen (**right** and **opposite**). But when the changes take place varies from person to person. So, if some of your friends are boasting because they are having to shave already or have bigger breasts than you, it's nothing to do with being clever, it's just the way they are made and soon you'll have caught them up.

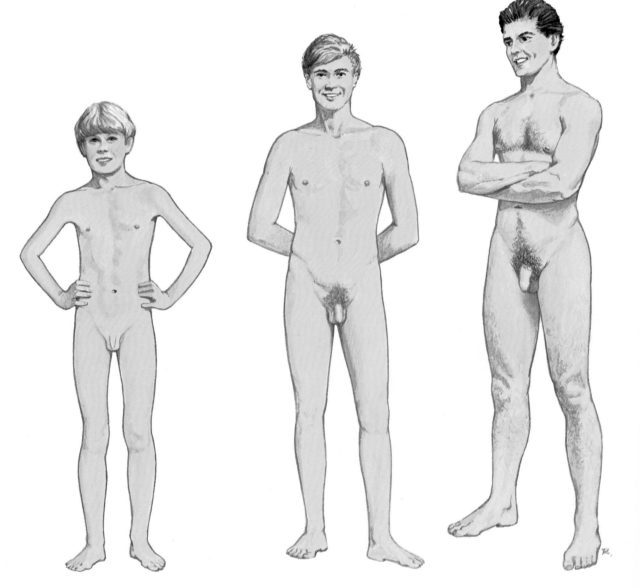

a monthly cycle. About every 28 days, one egg travels down from an ovary to the womb, a small bag shaped organ in their body, where a baby could grow. If the egg does not meet a sperm, it and the blood-rich lining of the womb are discarded before the next egg is released from the ovary.

While these physical changes are taking place, boys and girls often find themselves suddenly loving or hating people for no good reason. Sometimes they feel enormously happy or sad, energetic or lazy, also for no reason. This is because many powerful hormones are at work making their bodies adult. These chemicals act on the brain as well and so affect our feelings and moods.

◄When a woman becomes pregnant, the mammary glands in her breasts begin to change so they will produce milk to feed the baby. You may have seen a baby nuzzle its face into its mother's breasts even when she has clothes on. Instinctively, every baby knows where its mother's breasts are.

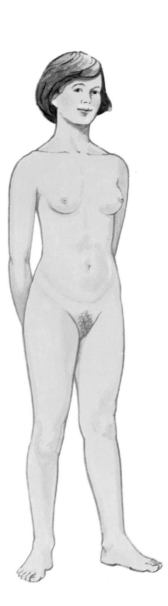

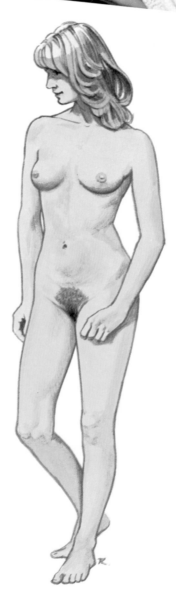

HEREDITY – WHO DO YOU LOOK LIKE?

The next time you are with a new baby, listen to the questions people ask. They're sure to say things like: does he have his father's eyes? I think she takes after her mother's family. Will he be as tall as his grandfather? Her grandmother had red hair too. All these questions and statements are saying something about the baby and its parents and grandparents, perhaps something about aunts and uncles as well.

Genes and chromosomes

One of the important things about sexual reproduction is that because two cells from two different individuals must come together to start another new person, all the characteristics of each parent will have a chance to be combined in a new way. Things we notice like hair colour, height, the shape of a nose or ears thus seem to pass from generation to generation in a family. Things that affect internal organs can also pass. This happens because within each cell is a set of instructions. They are called genes and they are printed on the chromosomes, a pair of tiny thread-like structures within the cell. One chromosome from a sperm combines with one from an egg when a baby is being made. Human beings have 23 pairs of chromosomes in their cells. Long before we could see chromosomes through microscopes people knew that somehow *characteristics* passed from generation to generation but they did not know how. They usually thought it was something 'in the blood'.

Genes usually produce exact copies of themselves but sometimes a change occurs suddenly. This is called a mutation. Mutations are usually harmful but sometimes they can help a living being survive. A whole science has developed to study what genes do within the cell. It is called *genetics*.

◀Although this child has inherited some features of its parents, for example blonde hair like its mother, its genetic make-up is unique. The baby the mother is expecting will also inherit a unique genetic mix.

▼Genes are difficult to see, even under powerful microscopes. Fortunately, for scientists studying heredity the fruit fly has genes that are quite easy to see.

►This cell is about to divide. The chromosomes are the dark threads inside the nucleus.

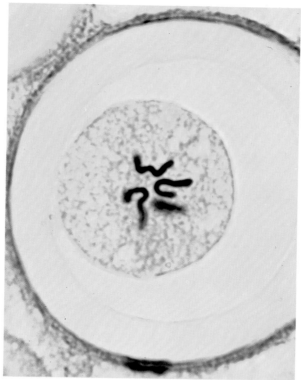

▼Identical twins like these two will have identical genes. The bond between twins is very strong – far stronger than between ordinary brothers and sisters.

GROWING OLD

The human body slowly wears out and this process is called growing old or aging. Someone may think of himself as quite young at 30. Really he has already begun to grow old. Not all parts of the body seem to grow old at the same rate, though. There is also a very great difference between individuals and also between people who live in different countries. So many things affect how fast we grow old: the work we do, the food we eat, where we live, how much exercise we get, and even our own ideas about how fit we are and what we can still do.

Signs of age

Some changes are common to all people as they grow older. The hair on the head becomes thin and grey. The skin of the face, neck, and arms becomes wrinkled and dull. Hearing becomes less sharp. Because the lenses of the eye can no longer change shape easily, spectacles must sometimes be worn to help sight. After women are about 50 they no longer have a monthly cycle and so cannot have babies. The joints of the knees and hips can wear out with age too, especially in people who have done a great deal of active sports. All the bones become more brittle. The most serious change is that the arteries which carry the oxygen-rich blood to the cells slowly become more narrow. If this happens in the brain, it may affect the way the mind works.

Scientists do not know why we age. Some think there is a kind of clock inside the body which slowly runs down. Others think that cells no longer make perfect copies of themselves and so organs become less good at doing their jobs. Others think that when some hormones are no longer present, aging begins. But what growing old means to one person can be very different from what it means

▲A centuries-old yew tree is still alive and healthy. Trees are the longest living things on earth.

▲The wrinkled face of an old Portuguese woman. Sun and wind have added to the aging process.

►Despite all the changes, Sir Winston Churchill at 80 (**right**) was quite unmistakably the same man as Winston Churchill aged 30 (**far right**).

▼Average and maximum recorded life-spans of a number of animals. The dark blue is the average and the light blue the record.

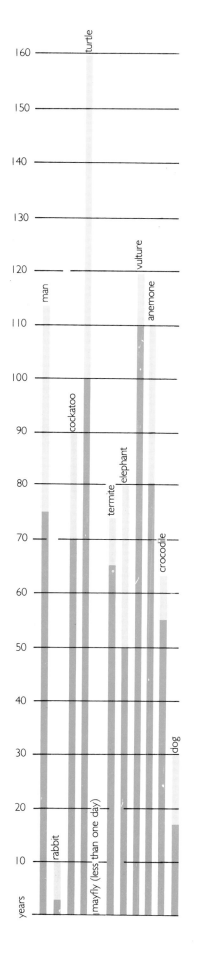

turtle

160

150

140

130

vulture

120

man

anemone

110

100

cockatoo

90

elephant

80

termite

70

crocodile

60

50

40

dog

30

20

mayfly (less than one day)

10

rabbit

years

to another. Many people in their seventies are busy, clear-minded, and strong. Some people in their fifties can be bent and frail. This is what a doctor or a scientist means if they say about someone 'Her chronological age does not match her biological age.' They are saying that the number of years the person has lived does not match the present condition of the organs of her body. The organs may seem much younger or older than one expects from her age.

▲'The same, only different' could describe us all as we grow older. But at least we do not have to grow old in public as Elizabeth Taylor and other film stars have to.

▲ This picture of a cancer in the left chest was produced by a machine that detects the vibrations made by the nuclei – control centres – of individual atoms. A computer decodes these vibrations and translates them into a picture that a doctor can use to discover what is happening deep within a living organ of the body.

Even after thousands of years of study and thought, we still have not worked out an answer to all our questions about the body and how it works. Some of the puzzles are not very important, like why hair grows grey or why do we have an appendix. Others are great questions. Many scientists and doctors are willing to spend their whole lives trying to find out just a small part of the answer to questions about why some body cells become sick and begin to destroy other cells. We still really understand very little about how the brain works. Although modern equipment has been able to tell us what many parts of the brain control there are still great sections of that organ which are deeply mysterious. We may have discovered a great deal about how people have babies but we still know very little about why many healthy people cannot have them when they want them. We understand what foods are good to eat and keep the body healthy but we are very puzzled about why some good foods, like milk, can make some people very ill. Because our bodies are so important, the more questions we ask the more we will learn. The more we learn the better we will be able to understand ourselves. The more we understand, the better care we will be able to take of our most important possession, our body.

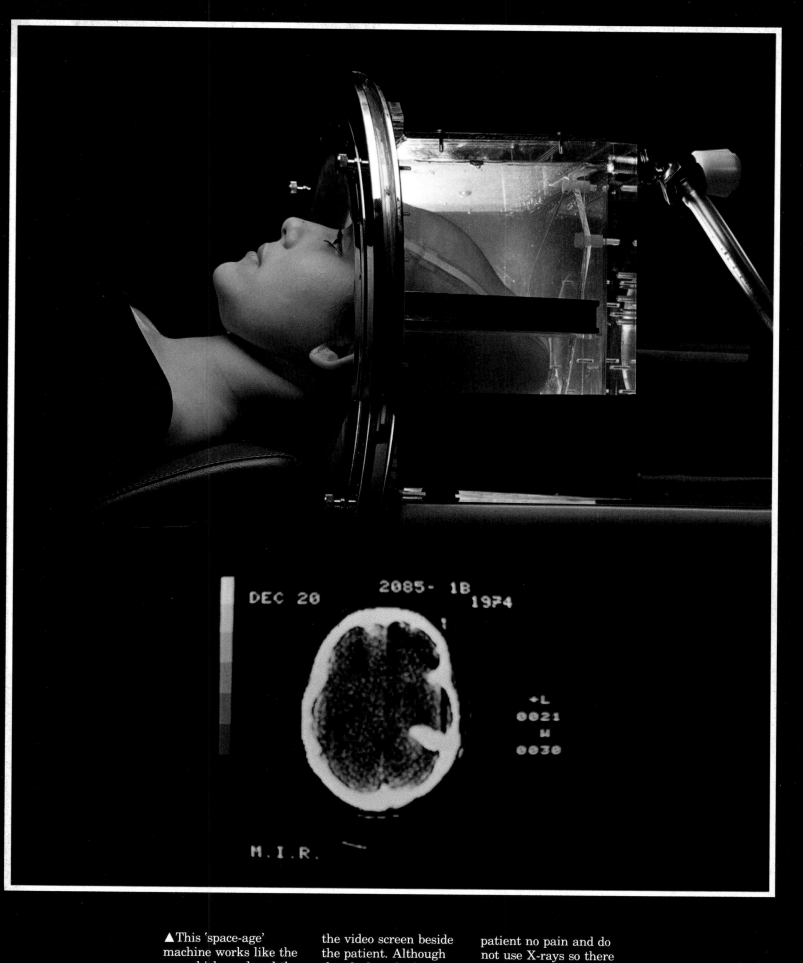

▲ This 'space-age' machine works like the one which produced the picture opposite – you can see the picture on the video screen beside the patient. Although they look rather frightening, these machines cause the patient no pain and do not use X-rays so there is no radiation danger.

▼This computerised X-ray scan through the middle of the patient's body uses colour coding in a different way to the thermograph on the right. The colours here vary according to the way different parts of the body resist X-rays. The roundish white patch is the spine.

▶All the blood vessels or vascular channels in our bodies give off heat. A thermograph takes a picture of what is happening deep within the body by registering the different heat levels from these channels. White represents the highest temperature and so the greatest amount of activity within the body. The colours go down through the spectrum to dark blue (cool) with a temperature difference of ½°C between each colour. A doctor looking at a thermograph checks to see if any area shows an unusual amount of heat or coolness. If there is such an area it indicates a problem. It shows that blood channels are either expanding to provide more blood to counteract infection (heat) or contracting because of a circulation problem (coolness). This thermograph shows a normal human head. The dark patch in the centre shows the patient had a very cold nose!

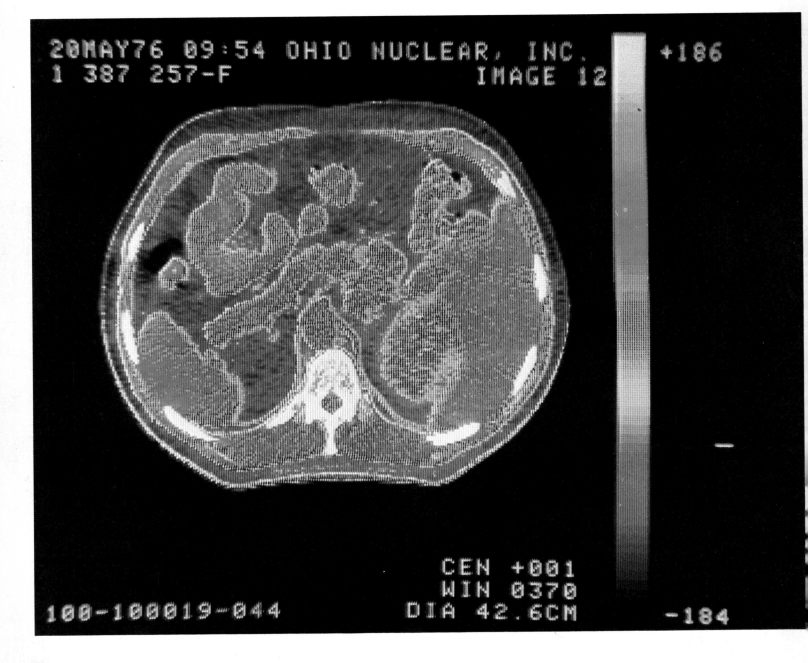

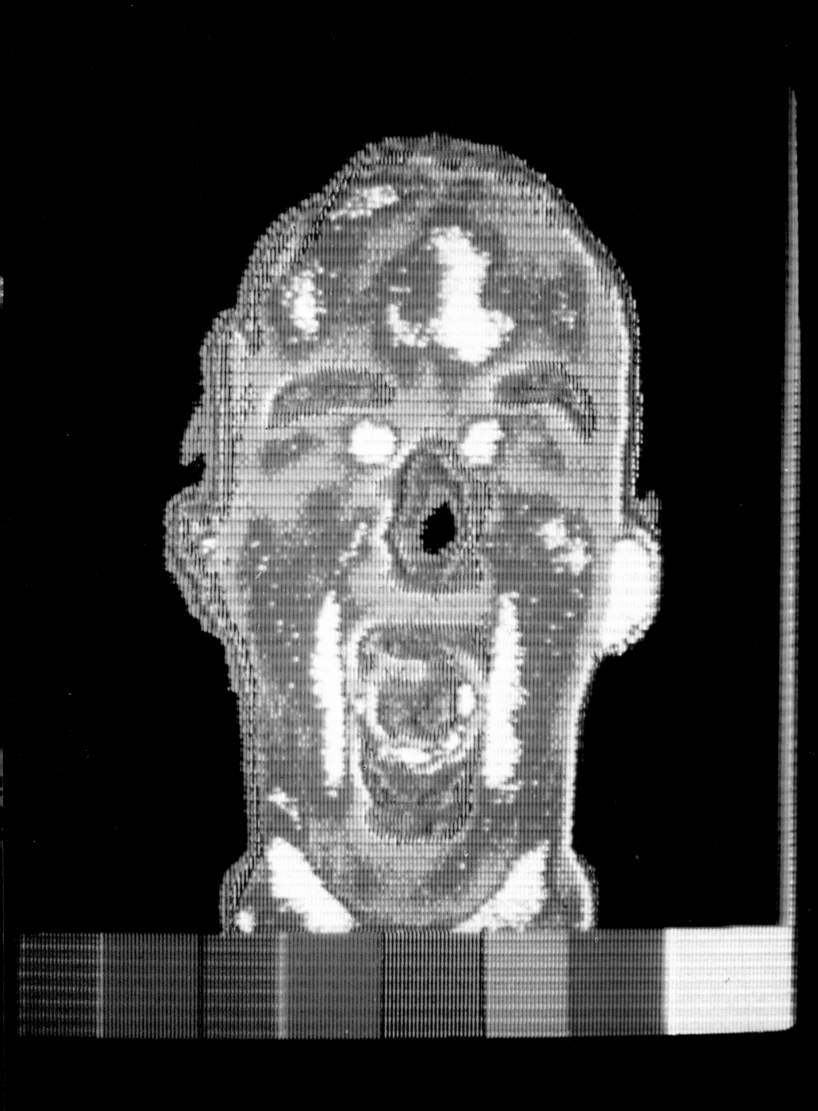

Anatomy The study of how living things are put together.

Antibodies Substances in the blood that fight disease.

Arteries Tubes carrying blood away from the heart.

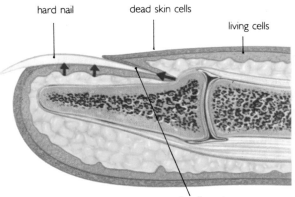

▼Nails grow from the top layer of skin – the epidermis. This has two layers, one living and one dead. The dead skin cells form a layer over the nail where it joins the living cells. This is the cuticle.

hard nail   dead skin cells   living cells

soft nail root

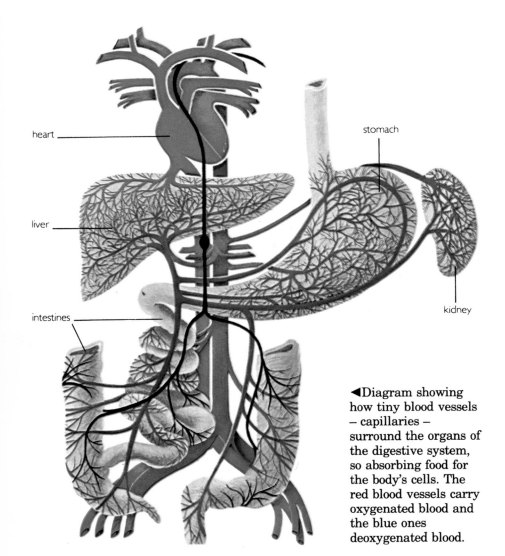

◄Diagram showing how tiny blood vessels – capillaries – surround the organs of the digestive system, so absorbing food for the body's cells. The red blood vessels carry oxygenated blood and the blue ones deoxygenated blood.

heart

liver

intestines

stomach

kidney

Capillaries The smallest blood-carrying tubes in the body.

Carbohydrates Foods that chiefly give us energy.

Carbon dioxide A waste gas made when oxygen is used by the cell.

Cell The smallest unit of life.

Characteristic A noticeable feature of a person such as size, colour of hair, shape of ears, etc.

Digestion Changing the food we eat into chemicals our cells can use.

Dissection Cutting open a plant, animal or human being to find out how it is put together.

Electrical impulse A beat of electricity, like the beat of a drum; a very short burst of electricity coming again and again.

Electron A powerful but very small part of an atom.

Fats Foods that give us energy and some building materials for our cells.

Female Having to do with girls or women.

Fluid A damp substance that can be thin, like water, or thick, like honey.

Gas A substance we usually cannot see or touch which fills the spaces between things. There are many kinds of gas. Air is a mixture of gases.

Genetics The study of how the coded instructions within a cell work to pass on characteristics.

Glands Organs that make special chemicals for the body.

Hormones Chemicals made by glands. They give instructions to many parts of the body.

Instrument Something we use to help us

do something or find out something. A knife is an instrument we use to cut food with.

Intestines Tubes where digestion takes place.

Male Having to do with boys or men.

Membrane A special envelope of a cell or organ.

Molecule A group of atoms, a tiny part of a chemical.

Mucus A sticky fluid produced by some of the lining cells in the body. It usually protects other cells from harm.

Nervous Having to do with nerves, the special cells that carry messages to and from the brain.

Organs Important parts of the body carrying out special work.

Oxygen The gas all things need for life.

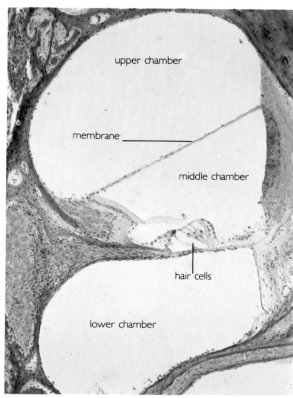

▲Everyone has different fingerprints. The ridges of the skin make many patterns possible, these are just a few.

▲The three chambers into which the cochlea of the ear is divided.

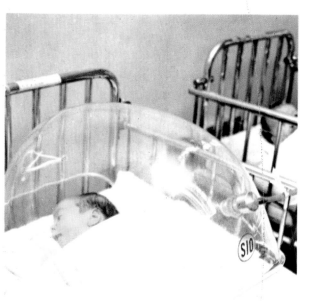

▲When a baby is born it has to adjust to breathing air instead of using its mother's supply of oxygen. If it has difficulty in making this adjustment it may be put in an oxygen tent. This will make breathing easier until the baby can cope on its own.

Physiology The study of how the parts of a living thing work together.

Proteins Foods that chiefly give us building material for the cells.

Reproduction The way a living thing makes another living thing.

Respiration Taking oxygen in and putting carbon dioxide out; this happens in all cells.

Systems A group of organs working together in one process.

Tissue A group of the same kind of cells doing the same job.

Veins Tubes carrying blood to the heart.

Vessels Tubes carrying fluid in the body.

INDEX

Acknowledgements
AP, BFP, Ron Boardman, British Petroleum Company, Julia Brown, Camara Press, Bruce Coleman, Douglas Dickins, Patrick Eager, Sally and Richard Greenhill, John Hillelson Agency, Roger Hyde, Archivio IGDA, Kobal Collection, Leeds Royal Infirmary, Chris Lund, University of Minnesota, Ken Moreman, NHPA, Popperfoto, Rank Research, Rex Features, Royal Postgraduate Medical School/Dr SM Lewis, Science Photo Library, John Watney.